The New Strategic Direction and Development of the School

Key frameworks for school improvement planning

Second edition

Brent Davies and Linda Ellison

RoutledgeFalmer
Taylor & Francis Group

LONDON AND NEW YORK

First published 2003
by RoutledgeFalmer
11 New Fetter Lane, London EC4P 4EE

Simultaneously published in the USA and Canada
by RoutledgeFalmer
29 West 35th Street, New York, NY 10001

RoutledgeFalmer is an imprint of the Taylor & Francis Group

© 2003 Brent Davies and Linda Ellison

Typeset in Sabon by
HWA Text and Data Management, Tunbridge Wells
Printed and bound in Great Britain by
TJ International Ltd, Padstow, Cornwall

British Library Cataloguing in Publication Data
A catalogue record for this book is available from the British Library

Library of Congress Cataloging in Publication Data
A catalog record for this book has been requested

ISBN 0–415–26992–X (hbk)
ISBN 0–415–26993–8 (pbk)

The New Strategic Direction and Development of the School

Schools will not be able to continue to improve unless they move away from an over-concentration on the short term and focus onto the strategic nature of planning and development. The more targets, the less the effects – what we need is strategy and sustainability. This book links school improvement planning and strategic development for leadership enchancement as well as for management accountability.

Short-term planning, in the form of target-setting plans aimed at improving standards, has gained increasing importance. While the book agrees that this is necessary, it puts forward the view that short-term planning is not sufficient for the longer-term development of the school. Sustainability and strategic development are of critical importance and for these the authors believe that a more holistic approach to planning is necessary. To that end, this books links short- and longer-term planning in a framework which supports the strategic development of the school.

The authors are national experts in the field and in preparing this text have worked extensively with headteachers, deputy headteachers, governors and those participating in NCSL and masters programmes in educational leadership and management.

Brent Davies is Professor and Director of the International Leadership Centre at the University of Hull.

Linda Ellison is Senior Lecturer in Educational Leadership at the University of Nottingham.

School Leadership series

Series editors: Brent Davies and Linda Ellison

The New Strategic Direction and Development of the School
Brent Davies and Linda Ellison

School Leadership for the 21st Century
Brent Davies and Linda Ellison

Effective Change in Schools
Chris James and Una Connolly

Effective Leadership for School Improvement
Alma Harris, Christopher Day, David Hopkins, Mark Hadfield, Andy Hargreaves, and Christopher Chapman

This book is dedicated to Katy Ellison

Contents

Figures

Tables

Contributors

Authors

Dr Brent Davies is Professor of International Leadership Development and Director of the International Leadership Centre at the University of Hull. He is also Special Professor at the University of Nottingham. Brent spent the first ten years of his career working as a teacher in south London. He then moved into higher education and now works exclusively on leadership and management development programmes for senior and middle managers in schools. He has published extensively with over fifty books and articles and his recent books include *School Leadership for the 21st Century* and *The Handbook of Educational Leadership and Management*. Email: b.davies@hull.ac.uk

Linda Ellison is a Senior Lecturer in Educational Leadership at the University of Nottingham. Linda has worked with a great many UK teachers and schools, and with school principals and teachers in and from a variety of countries including Hong Kong, Australia, New Zealand, the USA and the Caribbean. She has wide experience of developing and teaching on award-bearing CPD programmes for teachers, headteachers and other public sector workers. She is joint series editor, with Brent Davies, of Routledge's School Leadership and Management series. In addition, she has written nine books on school leadership and management and has published widely in academic and professional journals. Email: linda.ellison@nottingham.ac.uk

Case Study contributors

Barbara J. Davies has extensive experience in primary school leadership and management. After graduating from Oxford University, Barbara taught in primary schools in Oxfordshire, West Germany and West Sussex. She took up her first headship in West Sussex followed by her second in North Yorkshire. She was a Senior Lecturer at Bishop Grosseteste College in Lincoln working in initial teacher education before specialising in leadership and management in the primary sector at the University of Lincolnshire and Humberside, where she was a course leader for a Masters degree in leadership and learning. Subsequently she returned to primary headship as headteacher of Tuxford Primary and Nursery School in Nottinghamshire before taking up her current post as headteacher of Washingborough Foundation Primary School in Lincolnshire. Barbara gained a masters degree in Educational Management in 1994 and is currently completing her Doctorate in Educational Leadership at the University of Hull. Her thesis is focused on strategic leadership and planning in schools. She has published a number of books and articles in the field of educational leadership. Email: barbara.davies@washingborough.lincs.sch.uk

Peter Dawson began teaching in the science department at Brayton High School as a late entrant from an industrial career. He became a senior manager and led the TVEI in the school in the late 1980s. Peter became an advisory teacher in North Yorkshire working with primary, secondary and special schools and was then promoted to science inspector. Subsequently he moved to the City of York where, as Senior Adviser, he has responsibility for, amongst other things, science, monitoring and evaluation and school improvement planning as well as the secondary phase of education. He has contributed to courses and programmes on strategic leadership and quality assurance and was a visiting lecturer at the College of Ripon and York St John. He has had books and articles published in the area of science and environmental education. Email: peter.dawson@york.gov.uk

Angela Jensen trained as a primary teacher at Christ Church College, Canterbury and taught in a number of primary schools in London. After deputy headship and acting headship of St Thomas' Primary School in Hackney she joined the English advisory team in Waltham Forest and then moved to Wiltshire in 1992 to head the Professional

Development Centre and work as an advisory head teacher. For the past eight years Angela has been a link adviser for a group of primary schools in Swindon and worked with school leaders across all phases developing school self-evaluation and school improvement planning. Angela gained an advanced diploma from the Institute of Education in London and then a masters degree in 1991. She is currently undertaking a doctorate in Educational Leadership at the University of Hull. She has had several articles and LEA guidance documents published on a range of subjects including language, school self-evaluation, improvement planning and work with gifted and talented pupils.
Email: a.jensen@swindon.gov.uk

Ray Watkin's teaching career began in 1968 in Huddersfield, with further posts in secondary schools in Sheffield and Wakefield before taking up his first headship in Buckinghamshire in 1988. His second and current headship is in Coventry at Whitley Abbey Community School which he took up in 1993. He obtained his MEd, with distinction, from Leeds University in 1982. With publications in freshwater molluscan ecology, science education, special needs and co-author of a GCSE biology skills book, headship shifted his focus into leadership and management. Ray is currently completing his research dissertation into issues around inclusion and the leadership and management of a multi-agency team approach to engage hard to reach young people, for the International MBA in Educational Leadership at the University of Hull.
Email: watkin.uk@virgin.net

Foreword

Professor David Hopkins

During the past fifteen years, development planning has established itself as a key strategy for school improvement. In England in 1989 when the then DES issued its first advice, development planning was regarded as a means of helping schools manage the extensive national reform agenda, and to enable the school 'to organise what it is already doing and what it needs to do in a more purposeful and coherent way'. Given the amount of change schools and teachers were expected to cope with in the late 1980s and early 1990s such a strategy was widely welcomed.

This is not to say that development planning is a panacea. As an approach to school improvement, development planning has attracted its fair share of critics. Some have been concerned about its apparently bureaucratic and prescriptive character; its tendency to distort the nature of educational change and its 'hyper-rationality'; its lack of a management and strategic dimension; and its inappropriateness to some school settings and certain types of change imperatives. I have some sympathy with these concerns and was pleased that in their first edition of *Strategic Direction and Development of the School,* Brent Davies and Linda Ellison adroitly managed to articulate an approach to school development that avoided these pitfalls. In so doing they produced a book that spoke directly to the strategic needs of school leaders at a time when the reform agenda in England was characterised by what some have termed 'informed prescription'.

The new edition of the book comes at a similarly opportune time. 'Informed prescription' was an important and necessary stage in a long-term, large-scale reform effort, but such centralised reform strategies have difficulty in delivering the confidence, innovation and creativity that are so necessary for the knowledge society. The phase of reform we are entering will obviously still require some elements of 'informed prescription', but it will also have to be increasingly blended with an emphasis on 'informed professional judgment'. This will require teachers, heads and governors to be driven by a vision of what the school can be, and this is why this new edition of Davies and Ellison's book is so important. Many leadership theories and practices look backwards rather than forwards, but not those of Brent Davies and Linda Ellison. They argue that, because of increasing external demands and the uncertainty of events, school leadership has to be futures oriented and strategically driven.

Their new book seems to me to emphasise three key characteristics of school leadership that is futures oriented. The first is an articulate vision for the future of the school based on the values and beliefs to which the school community is committed. Second, is an ability to scan the environment for futures trends and directions and to adapt or work with them to help develop the school's internal purpose. Third, is the capacity to manage the change process. This requires skills such as the ability to generate trust, to diagnose the state of the school, to plan into the medium-term and to give people the confidence to continue.

Davies and Ellison's book also stresses that leadership needs to be strategically driven. Schools are currently facing two kinds of pressure. The first is that of development. Schools cannot remain as they now are if they are to implement an ambitious reform agenda. The second pressure is that of maintenance. Schools need to maintain some continuity with their present and past practices, partly to provide the stability which is the foundation of new developments and partly because the reforms do not by any means change everything that schools now do. There is thus a tension between development and maintenance. Strategic leadership, as Davies and Ellison demonstrate, is therefore about both ensuring maintenance and supporting development.

The focus on futures thinking and strategy is at the heart of Brent Davies and Linda Ellison's new book. It is the articulation of these themes that makes *The New Strategic Direction and Development of the School* such an important resource for all school leaders as we progress into a new phase of educational reform.

Preface

This book comes at an appropriate time in the evolution of planning approaches in school. Very considerable work has been done in schools on what was called school development planning and is now increasingly referred to as school improvement planning. However, there is much confusion when it comes to setting that short-term planning in a broader medium- to longer-term context. For example, as part of our research, we found this statement in an Ofsted report:

> From this informed base, *good strategic planning is undertaken.* The school improvement plan is comprehensive and has a clear focus on raising standards for Years 1 and 2 and sustaining standards for Year 6. Currently, *the plan does not run for more than a year.* (our italics)

This obviously shows little or no understanding of the nature of strategy. Strategy involves focusing on broad developments over a three- to five-year period and not simply extending the detail of an incremental one-year plan. Considering strategy as strategic thinking or as a strategic perspective, rather than as a linear planning process, is a valuable approach. This has been a common theme with the headteachers and deputy headteachers with whom we have worked. There is awareness that it is simply not possible to keep working harder at short-term incremental change and a broader medium- to longer-term view is needed. This is not only necessary at the medium-term strategic level but should also extend to incorporate longer-term futures thinking. This is seen in a number of futures-oriented groups such as the 2020 visioning work of the Specialist Schools Trust (SST) and initiatives from the National College for School Leadership (NCSL). To think outside 'the box' of the normal framework and look at broader economic, social and technological trends is one of the keys in moving from a management to a leadership perspective. There are those who would keep headteachers and deputy headteachers on a more reductionist diet of knowledge. Thrupp (2002) on criticising Caldwell's futures thinking proposes that 'Caldwell's (1997b) suggested "seminal reading" for the school leader is instructive: Peter Drucker's (1995) *Managing in a Time of Great Change*, Bill Gates' (1995) *The Road Ahead* .... Are these really the best bedtime reading for our school leaders? We should be recommending books which are far more educationally focused' (p. 12). While it would be simple to dismiss this view as patronising or arrogant, or typical of old-style sociologists, this is not our view. Such views are cause for considerable concern; they encourage a narrow focus for leadership and do not acknowledge the need to set education and educational leadership in a broader context. Drucker's book (Drucker, 1995), unlike many sociology of education or educational research books, is both accessible and meaningful. It provides a stunning critique of global trends that have impacted and are impacting on our lives. Ironically, Bill Gates and his Microsoft Corporation (despite being demonised as evil American capitalists) have probably been the major force in providing a more accessible and inclusive educational resource than has been previously possible. Shouldn't we hear what revolutionaries like Bill Gates are thinking? While education should be a broadening and not a narrowing process, so it is the same for educational leadership. Leaders are not only concerned with skill transfer for their pupils but should be interested in the sort of world that they will be living in and the type of skills and abilities which they will need to enhance their life-chances. So broader futures thinking is vital if we are to develop more effective leadership in schools.

We have made this new edition of the book far more focused than the first edition (and its reprints). We have taken on several of the ideas and comments from the many heads we have met on courses and at conferences and through individual planning consultancy exercises which we have undertaken in schools. Many of the comments encourage us to keep the model simple and support the idea of giving practical examples showing how organisations undertake planning. To this end, we have completely restructured and rewritten the chapters on futures thinking, strategy and strategic analysis, and action planning. In particular the importance of strategic intent and strategic conversations as a means of building capacity are emphasised as this has been a constant theme in our research findings. In our research, we have worked with many primary and secondary schools and a significant number of local education authorities (LEAs). We have drawn on this experience and include in the new book three case studies. We are grateful to Barbara Davies for sharing her primary school planning practice and to Ray Watkin for providing examples from his secondary school practice. Peter Dawson at York LEA created an excellent planning advice framework which Angela Jensen of Swindon LEA developed, and we are grateful to them both for the LEA model. These primary, secondary and LEA examples provide real-life examples of planning in practice in the education sector.

What has been satisfying about our work is that schools have found the three-strand planning model an invaluable framework through which to analyse their own planning processes, structures and documentation. However, even more significantly, they have been able to take on that framework, adapting, and amending it to build their own frameworks. This is the exact purpose of the new edition: to provide a framework that enables practitioners to reflect on their own planning practice, to review the case examples we provide and then to build their own planning models and approaches.

The challenge of planning is twofold. The first is to ensure that it builds on the short-term action planning frameworks of school development/improvement planning to encompass a longer time frame. This is a key factor in building sustainability into school development. There is a danger that short-term improvement planning while leading to increased performance will not be sustained. Barbara Davies (2003) puts forward the conceptual framework to link the importance of strategic and operational planning shown in Figure 0.1.

This matrix is perceptive in that it shows the critical importance of successfully developing both a strategic and an operational approach. While ineffective short-term planning combined with ineffective strategic planning will lead to obvious failure, good strategic planning without effective short-term planning will not lead to success. For sustainability, good short-term and strategic planning need to be combined. This is shown in the upper right hand quarter of Figure 0.1. Our planning model puts forward the idea that the backcloth of futures thinking, combined with strategic and action planning, will create a school that can be both immediately viable and sustainable in the longer term.

This leads onto the second challenge, that of integrating the different strands of planning. While in the book we talk about a futures, strategic and action perspective on planning, it is important to consider these

		Ineffective	Effective
Operational Processes and Planning (SDP & Target Setting)	**Effective**	Functionally successful in the short-term but not sustainable long-term	Successful and sustainable in both the short-term and long-term
	Ineffective	Failure inevitable both in the short and long-term	Short-term crises will prevent longer-term sustainability
		Ineffective	**Effective**
		Strategic Processes & Planning	

Figure 0.1 Short-term viability and long-term sustainability (Davies, B.J., 2003)

as concurrent and integrated processes. One of the challenges of being a leader in schools is that at the same time as you are leading and managing the day-to-day activities of the school and relating that to the short-term planning framework, you are undertaking discussions to build capacity for the future. Thus, planning should not be seen as a segmented process but as an integrated one. Similarly, we do not see planning as a 'one-off' annual process but as an iterative process of review, feedback and development.

Government reforms and initiatives over the last ten to fifteen years have been focused on putting a 'floor' under educational standards. This has been achieved by establishing curriculum frameworks and testing. To make those effective, short-term planning in the form of target-setting plans aimed at improving standards has gained increasing importance. While we agree that these are necessary, we also believe they are not sufficient for the longer-term development of the school. Sustainability and strategic development are of critical importance and for these we believe a more holistic approach to planning is necessary. To that end, we hope this book links short- and longer-term planning into a framework which supports the strategic development of the school.

We hope the ideas developed in our first edition have been refined and developed by practice and research to provide schools with insights to develop further and refine processes and plans in their own context. We look forward to responses from schools which will contribute to the continuing development of our work.

Acknowledgements

We would like to thank the following for working with us and developing our ideas

Barbara J. Davies
Peter Dawson
Angela Jensen
Ray Watkin

In particular, we would like to thank the staff and governors of Tuxford Primary and Nursery School, of Whitley Community School and of York and Swindon LEAs for permission to reproduce their documentation.

We would also like to thank all the schools with which we have worked and whose staff have contributed to the development of our work.

Chapter 1

Introduction

In the first edition of this book we used the phrase 'the thicker the plan the less it affects classroom practice!' We still agree with this but we would now add that a school's response to an inspector should be, 'Sorry, we don't have a school development plan – that is reductionist 20th century thinking! What we do have is an holistic planning process.' Our ongoing work with schools suggests that the short-term school development planning process is well established and functioning effectively in most schools. However, there is also evidence from our research that this short-term planning is often becoming over-prescriptive and reductionist in its approach, not least in its need to respond to the pressure of OFSTED (Office for Standards in Education) inspections. We see the necessity to build on this short-term planning but to make it more streamlined and focused and, at the same time, to set it in a broader strategic framework.

Our model of planning considers that there are three interactive strands to the process as shown in Figure 1.1.

In this chapter we will outline the nature and dimensions of the model and its elements and then go on to describe how the chapters that follow will consider the detail of each strand of the planning process, with examples from schools and LEAs.

Futures perspective

We do not believe it is possible to write a detailed futures plan for a school. What we believe is important is that schools engage in a futures dialogue to develop a futures perspective. This then enables the futures context or framework in which the school is operating to inform medium- and shorter-term planning. It is also important to define what we understand by 'futures thinking' because there is a danger

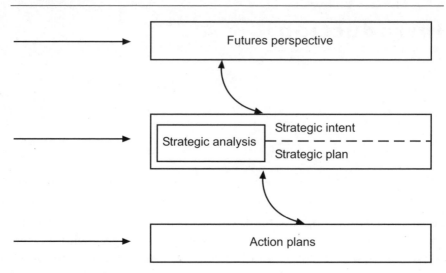

Figure 1.1 A model for school planning

that we may think of 'futures' as the year 2050 and a fictional world of Star Trek (although one of the authors thinks this is a documentary!). We believe that it is more useful to set the concept of futures thinking more deeply in the framework of the school and to link it to pupils. In business, the concept of a 'product life-cycle' is often used. An example would be the design of a car. Although a model may have a number of minor make-overs, it will be completely remodelled after five to ten years. How would we relate product life-cycle to the school sector? In schools, a child starting nursery school at the age of three in 2004 will not leave the primary school until 2012. Rather than thinking of future generations of children, what is the school planning to do for the children who have just started by the time they have reached the last year in the primary school? A similar analysis can be made in the secondary school for the eleven-year-old who has just started. What is the school going to provide for that student when she is eighteen? A consideration of these concrete examples puts futures thinking into a five- to ten-year framework. It also makes it real in terms of the child just starting a school and the responsibility that we have for that educational journey. In Chapter Two we explore the nature of futures thinking in the school more fully.

The strategic dimension

Strategy has been defined in a number of ways, and a detailed consideration of this will be undertaken in Chapter Three. In general terms, strategy should be seen as a medium-term activity, perhaps three to five years, and one which deals with broad aggregated data, rather than detailed plans. The concept of strategic flow (Davies and Davies 2003) summarises the nature of strategy used in this book as follows.

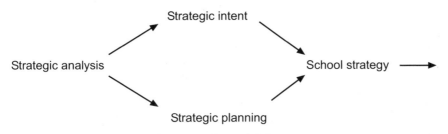

Figure 1.2 The strategic flow (Davies and Davies 2003)

This concept of strategic flow begins with the process of undertaking a strategic analysis of the school and its environment in order to determine possible courses of action. The course of action can be considered to fall into one of two broad categories: strategic planning or strategic intent. Strategic planning operates most effectively in an environment in which the school knows where it wants to go, understands how to get there, has the organisational capability and capacity to undertake the journey and will be able to evaluate the outcomes by some predetermined criteria. Strategic intent is effective in a situation where the school knows what it wants to achieve but does not, as yet, know how to get there. The school has to go through a process of building capacity and capability to understand fully the nature and dimensions of the strategic challenge and then has to work out how to establish a successful process for achieving those intents. The complexities around the different forms of planning for the medium-term are considered in Chapter Three. We have chosen to discuss futures thinking in Chapter Two and strategy in Chapter Three before considering strategic analysis in Chapter Four. It could be argued that analysis should come first but we felt it was better to establish the conceptual framework of futures and strategy to provide the contextual understanding for the analysis phase. Although some writers (Fidler 2002; Tsaikkiros and Pashiardis 2002) outline the strategic analysis, choice and implementation approach of Johnson and Scholes (1993), in practice, of course, schools do not go through a linear planning process. We believe that the process of planning is far more iterative and complex than it is often portrayed (Davies 2002a; Ellison 2002).

The operational dimension: action planning

We now use the term action planning for the short-term or operational stage of the planning process which sets out the proposals for a one-to two-year period. We believe that this terminology best reflects the nature of these shorter-term plans in schools and the need for clearly specified activities and outcomes. To reflect the DfES terminology, we are reserving the terms 'targets' and 'target-setting' for pupil outcomes and the process of specifying them.

When considering the style and focus of the short-term plan, there has been a shift in emphasis from input-based approaches to those which are output- or outcomes-based. This difference can be seen as follows. Early school development plans tended to be what, in economic terms, we would describe as input budgeting plans which, typically, had a series of *inputs* down the left-hand side of an A3 sheet such as:

Curriculum development
Staffing
Buildings
Equipment
Community links
Governors
and so on

Across the top of the sheet would be who does what, when, how, costs, evaluation etc. This contrasts with the move to output- or outcome-based approaches in the late 1990s and the first years of the 21st century which focus on specifying that which should be achieved. Now the increasingly common planning format is to have a series of outputs or outcomes down the left-hand side such as percentage increases in literacy and numeracy scores, attendance rates and so on.

As well as the nature and format of the plan, we would like schools to consider a realistic time period which can be covered by an action plan. We suggest that two years is appropriate for this level of detailed planning. Adding more and more years onto a detailed plan does not suddenly make it strategic. It may simply turn it into an unrealistic wish list. The disaggregated detail should not be extended in planning terms but, rather, it should be aggregated into broader information and stored as part of the strategic dimension.

The overall framework of a plan

It is important that, both in practice in schools and in this book, the terms used are clearly defined. We intend to use the generic term 'school improvement plan' as the overall framework. Within this, the futures element will be a five- to ten-year framework, the strategic dimension will take the school three to five years forward and the action planning stage will have a one- to two-year timespan.

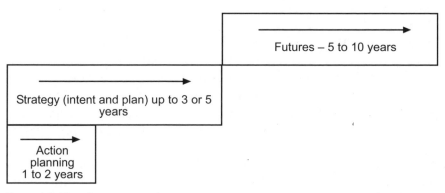

Figure 1.3 The planning time-dimensions

It is also critical that the three strands are not seen as isolated from each other and that there is a flow between them, an idea that is encapsulated in our model and that will be explored in greater detail later in the book.

A school improvement plan should therefore incorporate the following strands:

1 Introduction or context statement — the nature and dimensions of the school – age range of pupils, location etc.
2 Futures perspective — report of futures dialogue and perspectives developed in the school
3 Strategic dimension — i) strategic intent statement
ii) strategic plan
4 Operational dimension — action plan

In this book, therefore, we seek to establish new ways of thinking and operationalising school planning. The book is aimed at all those in leadership and management positions in schools who are reviewing and re-examining their planning processes. In particular, it should be an invaluable resource for those defined by the National College for School Leadership (NCSL) as 'established leaders' or those embarking on 'entry to headship' through the National Professional Qualification for Headship (NPQH) or through programmes such as 'New Visions', aimed at newly appointed heads. In terms of experienced headteachers ('advanced leadership' or 'consultant leadership' in NCSL terms) we see the book as a way of refocusing planning in schools from an operational management process, associated with traditional school development planning, to a much more holistic strategic process. For those readers undertaking Masters qualifications or EdD courses we hope to have merged the 'theory for understanding' and 'theory for action' elements of the traditional literature in the field of strategy and planning. It is hoped that governors of schools will continue to find this a key resource in developing their role in planning for the school.

The book is structured so that Chapters Two, Three, Four and Five examine aspects of our planning model, proforma for which are provided in the Appendix. Chapters Six, Seven and Eight present case studies which show how our model has been adapted or presented by a primary and a secondary school and by LEAs.

We are pleased that our publishers have invited us to contribute a completely new edition of this book after several reprints of the original edition. We have been gratified that many school leaders have used our approach and developed it by adding new ideas and incorporating their existing good practice. It has been by hearing about some of these modifications, and working with colleagues in schools, that we have developed our thinking and our model for this book.

Chapter 2

Building a futures perspective

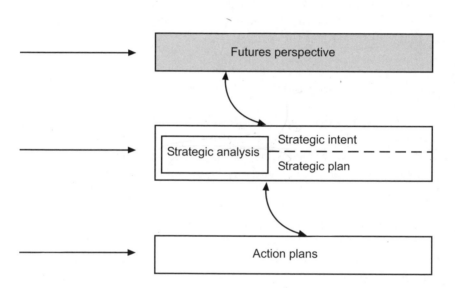

Introduction

The first dimension of our model of school planning involves creating a framework for futures thinking in the school. At the outset we would state the difficulty of writing a formal futures plan. Rather, we would recommend that 'futures thinking' develops through a 'futures dialogue' so as to build a 'futures perspective' in the school. The futures perspective can provide a 'backcloth' against which short-term and medium-term planning can be set. This requires the *leadership* capacity of 'looking outside' or 'looking to the horizon' which is fundamental to setting the direction of an organisation and contrasts with the *management* priority of co-ordinating current activities. Futures thinking involves the school leaders in standing back from the traditional operational and incremental thinking approaches and analysing broad global and national trends which are likely to impact on education over the next five to ten years and beyond. The leader must then start to build in the school the capacity or 'mindset' to interpret and understand the significance of these trends for the school. This is a radical agenda for school leaders. Peter Drucker, a management writer who is highly respected for his predictions of trends saw, a decade ago, the challenge as follows:

> What will be taught and learned; how it will be taught and learned; who will make use of schooling; and the position of the school in society – all of this will change greatly during the ensuing decades. Indeed, no other institution faces challenges as radical as those that will transform the school.
>
> (Drucker 1993: 209)

He set this in a more fundamental shift within society:

> Every few hundred years in Western history there occurs a sharp transformation ... Within a few short decades, society rearranges itself ... its world view; its basic values; its social and political structures ... We are currently living through such a transformation.
>
> (Drucker 1993: 1)

We see that some of this has partly come to reality and the pressure for change continues. This would suggest that schools need to develop the ability to identify and plan for fundamental changes in the way that they carry out their role. Schools are, however, places where the organisational history and culture make it notoriously difficult to bring about change. If we are to do more than respond to immediate policy changes or current crises we need to identify potential trends, consider possible future scenarios and, above all, build reflective learning communities which can adapt to whatever challenges or opportunities arise. This involves agreeing and living a set of values as a benchmark and building a set of learning skills so that opportunities can be shaped and taken rather than the school being the victim of unforeseen changes and events.

All organisations should see the need to reappraise fundamentally what they are doing as a result of changes in the global economy. Schools are no exception. The rest of this chapter will put forward ideas which we hope leaders will use to change mindsets so that schools can respond to the needs of the future. We look first, therefore, at the nature of the changes that we face and, second, we look at three perspectives which provide a vehicle to change 'mindsets' to enable staff to think about the future. At the end of the chapter, we suggest some ways in which schools might promote dialogue about trends which could affect schools.

The nature of the changes

When considering the changes that face education and the challenge of leading schools into a successful future, school leaders encounter two problems. The first of these is articulated by Hamel and Prahalad:

> So the urgent drives out the important; the future goes largely unexplored; and the capacity to act, rather than the capacity to think and imagine becomes the sole measure for leadership.
>
> (Hamel and Prahalad 1994: 4–5)

This tension is contextualised for headteachers in over a decade of educational reform and innovation during which they have been responding to multiple innovations, especially in the areas of centralised curriculum, assessment and inspection demands from central government. The 'urgent' agenda imposed on heads and the increasing accountability demands for managerial responses have left little time for reflection and school-based leadership solutions.

The second problem is articulated by Charles Handy:

> We are all prisoners of our past. It is hard to think of things except in the way we have always thought of them. But that solves no problems and seldom changes anything.
>
> (Handy 1990: 54)

An incremental approach to change and decision-making is deeply ingrained in our culture and to challenge current orthodoxy and think differently presents a considerable shift. It is important to spend time reflecting on the key changes that are impacting on schools and their environment. To support this, we will draw on Davies and Ellison (1999) and Davies (2002b) to outline eleven changes which are affecting schools and which will require consideration when building a futures dimension in the school planning process. These changes relate to: (1) the changing economic and societal contexts; (2) the changing tracks of educational reform; (3) the changing 'educational business'; (4) the changing tensions between autonomy and recentral-isation; (5) the changing impact of technology; (6) the changing use and misuse of information; (7) the changing nature and range of schools and their specialist character; (8) the changing understanding of the nature of 'learning'; (9) the changing roles and patterns of staffing; (10) the changing location and timing of learning; (11) the changing nature of equity in educational provision.

I   The changing economic and societal contexts

In an interesting review of the changes that are impacting on our society, Charles Leadbeater uses a provocative title to his book: *Living on Thin Air – the New Economy* (Leadbeater 1999). He outlines a useful way of categorising the changes that are impacting on the modern world by pointing to 'the three forces driving change in the economies of modern societies: *finance capitalism, knowledge capitalism* and *social capitalism*' (Leadbeater 1999: 5). Using these categories, it is possible to draw out implications for schools.

Leadbeater considers that *finance capitalism* 'is the disruptive power of deregulated, interconnected global financial markets' (op. cit. p. 5). Finance capital moves around the globe, seeking the best return, and large multinational companies move production from country to country, seeking the lowest production costs and, thus, significantly affecting employment patterns. Reich (1992) suggests that in modern economies the old primary, secondary and tertiary divisions of the economy and employment are being replaced with three sectors of jobs. First are those jobs at the local minimum wage (the 'Macdonald's jobs') which have to be undertaken locally and cannot be exported. Second are the traditional semi-skilled and skilled assembly jobs (car assembly, furniture assembly etc.) which are now rapidly declining in developed countries as companies relocate to lower-cost emerging economies. In the expanding third sector are the jobs in the new economy related to information, communication and technology (ICT). It is critical that schools upskill our children to be part of the expanding third sector or they will be forced into the minimum wage jobs because the second-level assembly jobs are being exported. However, the capacity to transfer information rapidly between countries can pose an additional threat in that many of the ICT-based third-sector jobs can easily be transferred to low wage economies such as the Indian subcontinent.

Knowledge capitalism relates to the shifting balance between 'tangible' and 'intangible' assets. Leadbeater makes the significant comment that:

> Across a wide range of products, intelligence embedded in software and technology has become more important than materials.... The steel in the latest luxury cars in the US costs $1000, the electronics cost $3000.
>
> (Leadbeater 1999: 9)

The significance of this comment is that it is knowledge that is the prime resource in the modern economy and society. Training for today's jobs will not be as important as educating young people with 'thinking skills' and the ability to work together collaboratively to create the new assets of the modern society. However, as some of that 'collaborative working' may take place in a virtual work environment across international and cultural boundaries, there are further implications for the formative experiences of young people.

Social capitalism is the 'glue' that holds societies and communities together. In a very powerful argument for supporting networks of social relationships that create social capital, Leadbeater comments:

> A trend towards inequality is deeply ingrained in modern society. Poorer people are less able than rich people to cope with the risks inherent in the global economy. To reverse this trend we need to invest in new institutions of social solidarity. That is the defensive case of social capital. There is a creative case as well. An ethic of collaboration is central to knowledge-creating societies. To create we must collaborate.
>
> (Leadbeater 1999: 13)

In the educational context, schools traditionally provided the 'intellectual capital' such as literacy, numeracy and scientific understanding, while the family provided the social capital. The change in employment patterns, the breakdown of traditional family groupings, the decline of religious practice and the growth of consumerism have all impacted on the social capital supporting the child. The change affects many schools so that they now need to provide the social, as well as the intellectual, capital for children.

2   The changing tracks of educational reform

One of the most original thinkers and contributors to the field of educational leadership and management over the last twenty years has been Professor Brian Caldwell at the University of Melbourne. His trilogy of books, written with Jim Spinks over ten years, *The Self-Managing School* (Caldwell and Spinks 1988), *Leading the Self-Managing School* (Caldwell and Spinks 1992), and *Beyond the Self-Managing School* (Caldwell and Spinks 1998), charts the developments of the global reform in this field. In his perceptive analysis of the reforms in the school sector, he describes 'tracks' of reform going through three stages:

> Track 1: Building Systems of Self-Managing Schools
> Track 2: Unrelenting Focus on Learning Outcomes
> Track 3: Creating Schools for the Knowledge Society
> (Caldwell and Spinks 1998: 11)

In Track 1, 'Building Systems of Self-Managing Schools', the systems include centralised curriculum, assessment and accountability together with decentralised responsibilities, including the control of resources, at the school level. This is certainly a process which we have witnessed in England with the National Curriculum, Key Stage testing, OFSTED inspections, and the publication of test and examination results imposed by central government, alongside the devolution of resource decision-making to schools. No one would doubt the increased 'formal' autonomy at the school level but many would suggest that 'over-regulation' and 'innovation overload' are now reducing significantly the individual school's ability to control its own affairs.

Track 2, the 'Unrelenting Focus on Learning Outcomes', is very evident within the UK system, with literacy and numeracy strategies being at the centre of the government's attempt to improve learning outcomes and test results at Key Stages 1, 2 and 3. Whether the 'shallow' learning, which is measured by replication in tests is accompanied by 'deep' learning and understanding remains to be seen (a point that will be developed later). However, there is little doubt that a 'floor' has been put under standards. The way in which the changes develop in the future will be critical. Will schools be given the freedom to explore the 'ceiling' of achievement or will they keep responding to increased targets (the floor) in the basic skills to the neglect of broader educational outcomes and achievement? Can governments provide a framework for schools or are they seduced into controlling the system by over-prescription?

Track 3, 'Creating Schools for the Knowledge Society', remains the main agenda item for the education system. In our work we seek to encourage a futures view that is educationally, ethnically and socially inclusive. Thus, while key skills are vital, we should not downgrade broader educational aims and awareness of other peoples and their cultures. Otherwise, the danger of a reductionist approach, as highlighted by a former Vice President of the United States, is all too frightening:

> I was recently on a tour of Latin America, and the only regret I have is that I didn't study my Latin harder in school so I could converse with those people.
>
> (Dan Quayle in Moe, Bailey and Lau, 1999: 11)

3 The changing 'educational business'

Davies and Hentschke (2002) examine the changing resource and organisational patterns that are impacting on education. To analyse these patterns, they pose three basic questions about education:

a) Who pays?
b) Who provides?
c) Who benefits?

The first of these, 'Who pays?', presents a rapidly changing pattern with an increasing reliance on multiple sources of revenue. In the education sector in general and schools in particular, leaders have traditionally relied on a small number of revenue sources, mainly state funding through Local Education Authorities (LEAs). Now this state revenue source is being expanded by the addition of the following categories: (a) donor sources, (b) parental sources, and (c) for-profit and not-for-profit business sources. Donor sources can be seen in the specialist school initiative in which schools that can attract sponsorship are then able to acquire significant funding from the government for the development of the specialism, such as technology, performing arts or sport. Parental contributions to the funding of education have changed radically with the introduction of tuition fees in the higher education sector and the increasing need to support school activities.

It is likely that the state-only funding and parent-only funding of school education will become a continuum, rather than an either/or situation. The involvement of the for-profit and not-for-profit sectors in education has taken a number of forms and is a rapidly increasing area. A very overt introduction of private capital is in the form of the Private Finance Initiative (PFI) which involves private companies raising the capital to build schools and then leasing the buildings to the operator (usually the LEA). The privatisation of 'failing schools', such as the former King's Manor in Surrey (now Kings College), so that a private company (in this case, a not-for-profit one, 3Es) is paid to run a school, based on certain performance criteria, can also be seen as introducing 'private' resources into the school sector.

The second question, 'Who provides?' has two interesting dimensions, (i) the changing organisational framework for the provision of services from an internal hierarchy to a market model and (ii) the changing mix and variation of providers of education and educational services.

(i) Schools themselves, or the LEAs that control them, have traditionally used their own hierarchical organisational structures to provide most of the services that they require. During the 1990s, a significant shift was seen to the outsourcing of school services so that there is now an increasing reliance on contracting-out within a market environment as an alternative to providing all educational services from within the school or LEA. This change has taken place through two mechanisms: first, the delegation to schools of their budgets (including staffing) and, second, the requirement within that delegation to engage in competitive tendering for the supply of goods and services. An additional driver for this change has been the increasing accountability and the decreasing resource base of the LEA.

Schools (and, indeed, local government) are, therefore, relying more heavily on contracting with other organisations to perform services that traditionally have been undertaken by employees within the school or LEA. Examples would be advice on curriculum and learning approaches, legal services and so on. The concept of outsourcing work is not new; it is a variant of the classic management decision as to whether to buy something or to make it. Indeed, one of the basic decisions that all organisations have to make is whether to use their own organisational hierarchy (internal staffing and organisation) or to use markets by entering into contractual relations with another organisation. Economists who study this topic (e.g., Williamson 1987, and Williamson and Masten 1999) argue that the only reason to create a firm is to provide a contracting relationship between employer and employee which is 'superior' to contracting in the marketplace. The change seems to be that, for some of its work, the school becomes an organiser of services, rather than a provider of those services.

(ii) Traditional educational institutions are now complemented by a wide variety of emerging providers of education and educational services. Whereas the traditional providers, schools and colleges, are largely public organisations, the emerging providers are largely private for-profit and private not-for-profit organisations. Traditional education institutions typically provide the full array of services expected, whereas emerging providers may serve either a comprehensive function (e.g. the running of a whole school) or pursue a more specialised niche. Many emerging education service providers see their ultimate market as national or even international, i.e. they are not constrained by the local political jurisdictions within which traditional education institutions have developed.

The changes in the sourcing of education are also leading to changes in the pattern of what is provided by whom. The school has traditionally established geographical domination by providing the whole range of educational services in an area. Thus, an all-ability school has made comprehensive educational provision for children within its local area. However, we see major counteracting forces emerging that fundamentally challenge the dominance of the local all-ability school. This challenge is led by the very significant growth of specialist schools. In England, the specialist schools initiative promotes a larger geographical catchment area which changes the nature of the school. Another challenge to local comprehensive provision is the privatisation of education services at the LEA and school level which can be seen as a revolution in changing the mix and variation of providers.

The third, and most significant, question, that of 'Who benefits?', presents an unsatisfactory response that 'the jury is still out' because determining the changes here is not very straightforward. Two key issues emerge in this new framework. The first is the need to adjust the criteria for school funding to include equity as well as effectiveness and adequacy. The second issue, the redefining of schooling as a commercial industry as well as a social good, involves a reconceptualisation of the role of government.

What are the implications of these three questions and their answers? It could be that the role of government is changing from a social welfare function to an economic investment function. The future may be one in which the government deals with the education 'industry' as it deals with other industries, for example by attracting it, fostering its growth, minimising its negative externalities and ensuring consumer protection, rather than seeing itself as the direct provider.

4   The changing tensions between autonomy and recentralisation

The significance of the changes that followed the 1988 Education Reform Act (DES, 1988) in England and Wales cannot be underestimated. While schools had significantly increased autonomy in relation to resources under forms of delegation (such as Local Management of Schools (LMS) and Grant Maintained Status (GMS)), they had enormous increases in central direction, control and accountability in the forms of a National Curriculum and centralised assessment combined with the OFSTED inspection 'regime'. We would consider this to be a change from a traditional input model of education to a centrally determined output model as shown in Figures 2.1 and 2.2.

The significance of these figures is that they show the reversal of the flow from an input-driven to a centrally determined output-driven and centrally controlled model of education. This has resulted in considerable tensions about what should constitute 'local management'.

The government reforms in terms of the replacement of LMS and GMS funding systems with Fair Funding (considered by some headteachers as an oxymoron!) have, for some, reduced school control. Indeed, the Standards Fund has significantly reduced the ability of schools to direct resources to areas they determine as priorities and has replaced it with central government direction of resources for its 'priorities'. It has, by channelling money through LEAs, augmented their role somewhat. In curricular terms, not only has *what* to teach but also *how* to teach been centrally determined by developments such as the literacy and numeracy strategies. These initiatives have reduced further schools' control of the education process. The danger is that the government becomes addicted to control. Schools are forced into compliance, regardless of their actual opinions and both the floor and the ceiling of educational standards are determined by central government.

There is a tension between compliance and performance. Excessive compliance reduces the scope for creativity and limits performance. It will also put undue emphasis on outcomes, with processes having to be ignored. Among these processes are 'thinking skills' and, despite

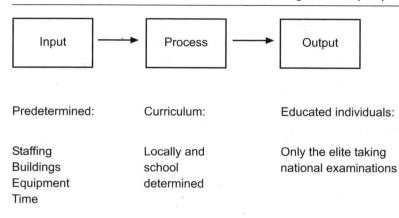

Figure 2.1 Traditional model of the educational process (Davies 2002b: 200)

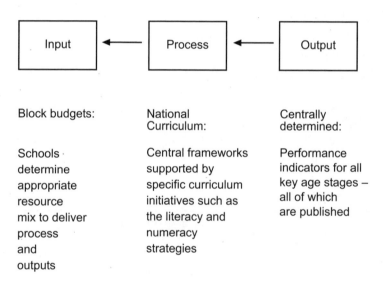

Figure 2.2 New model of the educational process (Davies 2002b: 200)

a former Chief Inspector of Schools not believing that they have a place in the curriculum, schools increasingly realise that a proper focus on thinking skills is vital in the pursuit of deep learning. The outcomes addiction also diminishes the central importance of a view of education that is wider and deeper than simple test results. The famous quote from Proverbs 28:18 'where there is no vision the people perish' has a ring of truth in it. Schools need time and scope to build and develop their own visions – they cannot be centrally imposed with a 'one size fits all' mentality. Indeed, Michael Fullan's (1993) concern that premature and externally imposed visions can blind us to effective improvement strategies is a powerful warning in this context. We now face the danger that the significant improvements in education will be put at risk by over-prescription and regulation, resulting in organisational and personal stress which is self-defeating for the education sector. We, like many others, recognise the tremendous improvements made in our schools and comments like 'bog standard comprehensives' from a government press spokesman are as inaccurate as they are offensive. Having established a framework for schools within which they can both operate and be held accountable, the government needs to trust the schools to deliver and must not demoralise them with further controls.

5 The changing impact of technology

The application of Information and Communications Technology (ICT) has been the most powerful change agent in the educational world over the last twenty years. However, has that change in learning technology fulfilled its potential and is it a change that will unite or divide our society? In assessing whether technology has fulfilled its potential, it is useful to use a categorisation of learning often articulated by our colleague John West-Burnham. He categorises learning in three domains shown as follows:

Table 2.1 Modes of learning

Shallow	Deep	Profound
Replication	Understanding	Meaning
Information	Knowledge	Wisdom
Experience	Reflection	Intuition
Extrinsic	Intrinsic	Moral
Compliance	Application	Challenge
Dependence	Independence	Interdependence

In assessing the changing use of technology for learning in schools, it is interesting to reflect as to whether we have moved from its application as an information source that produces shallow learning to its more sophisticated use to promote deep understanding or, indeed, whether there has been any profound learning involved. For the majority of our students, we would suggest that we are only just starting on a journey to deep and profound learning.

The assessment as to whether technology will unite or divide our society is too unclear to make at the moment, although we do know that ICT has the potential to bring both resources and educational interaction into every home. But therein lies the problem. Not every home can either afford, or may be inclined to support, the use of technology. Thus, children in supportive homes that have adequate resources are likely to be considerably advantaged against those that do not. The danger is that technology will widen the gap between the 'haves' and 'have nots' in our society. The change that is occurring in some schools, and needs to happen in all schools, is that they become learning centres providing that technology access and support outside the traditional school day and school year and for the whole community.

6   The changing use and misuse of information

Age-related test data can provide a treasury of material that can contribute to sustainable student achievement. However, in England, those data are being turned into information that is being misused by politicians to the detriment of students. It seems obvious that, if a key stage test highlights that a child does not understand some key concept or skill, then that test information should provide an agenda for that child's personal learning contract. However, the current approach is to provide generic 'booster' classes to ensure that children 'pass' the test so that government targets can be achieved. Surely we do not want to reinforce 'shallow' learning by encouraging children to replicate information to pass a test. What we need is deep learning to establish an educational base for that child to progress in the future.

There is also a further moral dilemma with the misuse of test results. While a lower result in key stage tests for a school may dictate the direction of future action for that school, it does nothing for that current child who has 'failed'. What is needed is to move assessment back from the output stage to the process stage where information about a child can alter what is being taught or how it is being taught to improve that child's performance. To do this we need to change the emphasis from 'assessment of learning' to 'assessment for learning'. While we would not disagree with external testing, the obsession for ever-increasing test outcomes may be counter-productive. It results in the neglect of the ultimately more rewarding, but more difficult, gathering of information for improving learning processes and this is likely to be detrimental to the whole educational process. We are likely to develop a position in which schools are educationally data rich, but information poor. What is needed is what Andy Hargreaves, while working with us in the Global Alliance for School Leadership, called a 'focus on deep learning and not just superficial performance results' (Hargreaves 2000: 14).

7   The changing nature and range of schools and their specialist character

From the 1970s until the mid-1990s, the rhetoric was that (other than in the selective secondary sector) schools were similar in nature giving 'equality of opportunity to all'. This was never actually the case because of resourcing, socio-economic factors and so on. The introduction of specialist schools and the subsequent expansion of this initiative to encompass a broader range of specialisms, along with increased opportunities for sponsoring this range (such as faith schools), has widened the provision on offer.

There are critics of diversity. For example, Husbands (2001) predicts that there will be problems following the introduction of specialist schools because 'Dismantling a comprehensive system of state education will be socially and educationally disastrous' (Husbands, 2001: 15). The danger is that moving resources around, as with specialist schools, may result in a situation that the specialist schools 'have sucked pupils, staff and innovatory energy from schools nearby' (op. cit.) which does little to solve the challenge of improving the learning opportunities of all our children. The challenge for educational leaders should be to focus on learning processes and the interconnectiveness of the curriculum, rather than on ways of tinkering with the administrative systems that we already have.

However, a much more radical transformation of school provision would be achieved by a loose–tight framework which provides for regulation with some flexibility. Greater flexibility has already been introduced into the curriculum and more is to come, especially at 14–19. It is to be hoped that greater flexibility will become available with respect to the requirements relating to adults and classes, pupil numbers and space and so on. This would be particularly useful in primary schools where the learning process could be more effective if certain requirements were relaxed.

An even more radical scenario has been described by Hargreaves (1997) who sees the school sector fracturing into four types of provision:

i. Private schools, forming an elite group based on traditional academic curricula
ii. Specialist schools, which are technology-based, providing high quality focused education
iii. Custodial schools, found largely in the inner cities and providing basic education only, thus keeping pupils off the streets
iv. Home schooling, expanding because of the support provided by the information revolution.

What does seem evident, whether it be the more radical scenario of Hargreaves or the more flexible application of the National Curriculum across all age ranges, is that diversity of provision is set to increase.

8   The changing understanding of the nature of 'learning'

There is now a greater understanding of how the brain works, leading to the design of more appropriate, varied and differentiated learning experiences and greater awareness (including self-awareness) of preferred ways of learning.

Key ideas in this field have developed significantly in the last ten years with Howard Gardner and his work on multiple intelligences being particularly influential. A good summary of his work can be found in *Intelligence Reframed – Multiple Intelligences for the 21st Century* (Gardner 1999). Gardner's numerous books have increased the understanding and debate about differentiation and reconceptualising the learning and teaching processes. This rethinking of learning has been shared by people such as David Perkins (1992) who writes perceptively in this field. Alistair Smith's work on 'accelerated learning' (1996) has developed a shift in thinking in many schools as to the nature of learning. These concepts have been developed extensively through research and development by people such as Philip Adey and Michael Shayer (1994) and David Leat (1999) and have been analysed and applied by school leaders such as Greg Barker (2003) and Derek Wise (2003).

The new learning technologies are putting the learner at the centre of the learning process, instead of the teacher, and are now starting to have a radical impact on pupils' learning. These technologies are not just seen in the school but are providing significant learning opportunities outside the normal school environment and structure. How children learn and, more importantly, how different children learn will be the main agenda for the next ten years. This contrasts with the suffocating micromanagement and accountability of the 'one size fits all' strategies and testing regimes seen recently in England.

9   The changing roles and patterns of staffing

The role of teachers and the skills and competencies that they display will have to be rethought over the next few years as they meet the challenge of transformed schools. Organising a learning programme and being the consultant on differentiated learning seems rather passive. We do not use concepts such as the teacher becoming a facilitator, but we regard him/her as being the 'wise' person who has the broader view and depth of knowledge, not only to deliver part of the portfolio, but also to take on the role of 'Director of Studies' for each child. It is important to consider that, while the technical competence to undertake a specific task is important, of greater significance are the generic competencies that individuals bring to a variety of situations. In teaching, while competence in a specific subject will remain important, a range of generic skills will take on increasing importance. Examples of these skills are: information retrieval; motivating students to work in self-directing learning groups; encouraging self-discipline so that learners take responsibility for their own work. Also, with the increase in the volume of information and the variety of information sources, an important range of skills will be those required to manage knowledge. People will need to work in and manage staff teams in order to utilise these resources instead of being isolated teachers. Rethinking by individuals of their roles as teachers also necessitates a readiness to change and encompass new developments. We would consider, in simplistic but nevertheless valuable terms, that half of the challenge of coping with change is a resource problem and the other half is changing 'mindsets'. The latter is probably more difficult to achieve! The McBer competencies (Davies and Ellison 1997a) of analytical and conceptual thinking allied to the 'flexibility' competency may be the ones which we need to develop as teachers rethink and regroup to meet the challenge of operating in the new environment.

Brent's uncle, who started work for a printing firm when he was 14, remained in the same job until he retired when he was 65, a pattern that is unlikely to be repeated by many workers in the future. Currently, the age at which individuals start work has increased and the age at which they retire has decreased, but employment in the future might involve periods on short-term contracts and holding a portfolio of jobs, a pattern that will continue after formal 'retirement'. Even in education, an individual will probably carry out a variety of roles over time. If the standard career track no longer applies, how do we manage staffing in schools? One way to think of reengineered employment patterns is to see teachers as individuals who contract to do specific jobs in the school for a specific time period for a reward package. If we have flexible budgets that adjust with the number of pupils, then staffing flexibility on the supply side is an organisational necessity. The challenge is to empower staff to be responsible for their own career and salary management rather than them being participants in a bureaucratic staffing regime.

In relation to the mix between teaching and support staff, much work has been done at the margins, but further opportunities can be created through a radical reappraisal of teaching and support staff roles which is beginning to take place. We could be considering different levels of teaching where 'master teachers' work with teaching assistants who have different salary structures. Utilising human and technical resources should become the task of the 'master teacher' in the search for increased learning outcomes. A new grade of standard and master teacher might be established. The most effective use of staff will require a freeing up of some of the legislation around adults and pupils to allow greater flexibility in deployment and a team approach to supporting learning. One of the challenges to be faced in such a team approach is the need to reward the performance of the team, rather than the individuals in it.

10 The changing location and timing of learning

As indicated earlier, the impact of technology on learning will lead to learners being able to access materials and support from a number of locations, both within and beyond the traditional school boundaries. This opens up extensive flexibility in the use of time and of physical resources.

Hargreaves (1997) suggests that parents with access to high quality technology will look increasingly to home schooling as an alternative to traditional schools. Why should a pupil go to a traditional school when he/she can attend a technology centre, work at home, engage in Internet tuition and so on? We would support those who argue that many of the key competencies for future success are people-related and that learning to work amongst and with a wide range of other people is one of the key features of a successful school. If technology does release learners from some of the traditional attendance needs, we believe that it is important that schools organise experiences in which interpersonal development can take place.

Barber's (1996) Pupil Learning Resource Credit and the Individual Learning Promise can be seen as an attempt to support flexibility and to bring back the responsibilities as well as the rights of parents. The framework that needs to be created is one in which there is a learning community responsible for children, rather than a community which passes all responsibility to the school. Indeed, the flaw in the school improvement and school effectiveness movements is that both see educational improvement solely through the school route. The rationale for a clear shift to the *learning* process is also proposed by Barber (1996) who points out that 'the implicit assumption behind school improvement is that the aspirations of every learner can be met within one school' (Barber 1996: 247–8). This is a clear rallying call to rethink the role of schools. Instead of being the sole providers they should be part of a wider learning network of providers and opportunities, with shared responsibility for pupil and adult achievement. The school can be at one of the pivotal points of this learning network but developing individual and community responsibility for education is as important as all the current attempts to improve schools. Giving all post-16 pupils a learning voucher or credit for *x* number of years education or *x* amount of resources to be used in a personal learning plan may be a more effective way of seeing education – as a process to be accessed flexibly instead of in terms of school attendance.

This flexibility is part of a culture in which individuals have several jobs in a lifetime and need access to regular skills and professional updating. Government policies and local initiatives are promoting wider access to educational opportunities and the re-entry to, or frequent moving into and out of, education. There is likely to be a greater use of schemes which blur the distinction between school and the workplace and which allow for re-entry into formal education.

Another facet of the scope for variation in *when* learning can take place is the use of the school year. Many people believe that the traditional school year, with its uneven terms and a long summer holiday, is a product of a bygone age, resulting in pupil boredom as well as pupil and teacher stress caused by the long terms and learning loss over the long summer break (although much of the research on summer learning loss has been carried out in the USA where the break is much longer). Internationally, year-round schooling, five-term years and shortened summer holidays have been used to give a more even pattern to the year and to avoid the disadvantages of the traditional pattern. There have been various attempts at reform in the UK, most recently proposals for a six-term year in England at the instigation of the Local Government Association (2000) but there is, already, a growing pool of leading headteachers with more creative approaches and successful patterns, for example, Derek Adam in Kent and John Lewis in Yorkshire (Lewis 1997). There is scope for further research on ideal patterns in particular contexts. What is the ideal length of a learning block? of a holiday? How can the pattern of the curriculum best be broken up? How can review and testing be most effectively carried out?

If the traditional school year is under threat, then the traditional school day is even more threatened as it is perceived to be part of a factory model of schooling which sees the mass knowledge transfer system as the best way to achieve universal literacy. New conceptualisations of the school day are necessary now that we have greater expectations of the education system and the responsibility for learning can been seen to be switching from the teacher to the learner. Indeed the expression 'school day' is itself becoming redundant. This rethinking of the school day is not just about altering timings. In designing a 'learning day', the concept of self-management should apply to the pupil as well as to the institution. How do we encourage and support the pupils to become responsible for directing and organising their own learning? An appropriate model can be achieved by switching the emphasis to one in which the learner organises a series of learning experiences which, while they may focus around the school day, are not solely constrained within it. A package of activities that the learner assembles to meet her or his individual learning needs might include, in addition to school attendance, a combination of work on technology-based activity outside the school and attendance at a homework support centre. It may also include educational resources at home in order to reengineer learning resources to be focused on the child and not on the institution of the school. In this context, teachers are helping to organise a school day that fits into an overall learning day. As such they are not just delivering the immediate lesson but are consultants on the most appropriate learning strategy for the individual pupil to employ in a variety of learning situations.

11   The changing nature of equity in educational provision

The moral question facing leaders in schools is how to give all the pupils in the school the best possible chance to fulfil their potential. Is it possible, if we offer differing provision to different groups, to ensure that they all have a fair share? Is it possible that if we can only benefit some pupils that we should do so, even though we know that it is impossible in the short-term to benefit everyone? In the stereotypical 'leafy suburb', resource levels at home mean that pupils not only receive their five or six hours of school tuition but can have another five or six hours uninterrupted Internet or other technology-based support on their own computer at home. If we take a failing school (as identified by the government) in a deprived inner city area, not only is the five or six hours of school-based learning inadequate, but pupils are unlikely to have the additional technology support at home. A double educational negative! Consider the scenario which follows.

A new headteacher is appointed to the school and decides not only on a plan to improve the teaching and learning but also to attack the technology gap. To do this she obtains sponsorship to buy some multimedia computers and to pay for staffing by IT experts. She charges all the pupils attending after school £1 for the session. She knows that not all the pupils can come – so she benefits the motivated and the ones able to pay rather than the unmotivated and those with limited funds. Progress in provision in the future is likely to come through such initiatives where there is benefit to some pupils but not all. Is that fair? Is any gain worth it? In fact, the early gains can often lead to further financial support which can then benefit a wider range of pupils.

These types of discussions are likely to occupy us as we move forward on diverse fronts at differing rates as the monolithic 'one size fits all' culture is replaced by individual initiatives and diversity of provision. This is a very simple example of how changes throw up major equity issues. Far more fundamental equity issues are brought to our attention by Hargreaves' (1997) analysis of the four types of school, especially the 'custodial school'. One of the key functions of the leader in this rapidly changing environment is to reassess and articulate the values which guide and underpin the school so that actions are consonant with these.

Concluding thoughts in relation to the changes that we face

These changes and trends are possible developments that educational leaders should seek to understand but, more importantly, the leader and the school should build into their planning the appropriate structures and processes to develop the capability for what the surfers call 'looking outside'. This involves the surfer looking to the horizon, searching the small or medium waves for the one or two significant waves that it is worth riding. 'Looking outside' in education involves monitoring the trends and developments to pick out the significant ones. It is then worth spending time exploring these and building the organisational capability to understand them in order to inform strategy.

How can a school begin to move forward in developing a futures perspective? We suggest that leaders should spend some time considering how to change mindsets in schools to increase willingness and capability to engage in a futures dialogue.

Three perspectives on changing mindsets

How do we take a fresh look at our situation? Three useful perspectives are provided by, reengineering (Hammer and Champy 1993), left and right brain thinking (Dent 1995) and the Sigmoid curve (Handy 1994).

Reengineering

Hammer and Champy (1993) first articulated the concept of reengineering in 1993 in order to explain the type of rethinking that was necessary in organisations to deal with the radical change in the nature of the global market. We consider that, in a school setting, reengineering has four elements: the *fundamental rethinking* and *radical redesign* of *learning processes* to achieve *dramatic improvement* in performance.

It is worth spending a little time unpacking each of these elements. First, reengineering is about fundamental rethinking. It avoids the incremental approach and starts with the proverbial 'clean sheet of paper' to reconceptualise the processes and their context. This links into the second element, that of radical redesign. Reengineering makes the assumption that past and current processes are inadequate so, while it is important to research why they are inadequate, more emphasis should be given to radical new solutions. Third, there is the key aspect of processes within organisations (which, in educational terms, would equate to learning processes). Hammer and Stanton (1995: 17) consider that:

> The verb 'to reengineer' takes as its object a ... process and nothing else. We reengineer how work is done, how outputs are created from inputs. We cannot and do not reengineer organisational units.

The reengineering of processes is at the heart of the concept of reengineering. Very often we are concerned with restructuring in the belief that it will effect change, rather than focusing on the processes that underpin the restructuring. For example, a secondary school may restructure fifteen departments into four faculties. However, that restructuring will not have any impact on the learning processes of the children within the new grouping. Similarly, in the primary school restructuring from head of infants and head of juniors to Key Stage 1 and Key Stage 2 co-ordinators will not necessarily have any effect on the learning processes of the children within those groupings. The example of the government limiting class size in Key Stage 1 to 30 pupils will not dramatically improve the performance of those pupils. Children who do not learn effectively in a class of 32 will not necessarily learn more effectively in a class of 30. What is needed as well as restructuring class size is a fundamental reengineering of the way those children learn and are taught. This concentration on learning processes is the focus of the 'brain based learning' or the 'new science of learning approaches'. For school improvement to be sustainable we need to concentrate on the learning process of children and how those learning processes form a culture of learning within a school. It would have been better for schools to have been funded on class size of 30 but been allowed to decide, according to actual learning needs, the appropriate class size.

The fourth element, dramatic improvement, is concerned not with making things five or ten per cent better but with achieving dramatic leaps in performance. This will only occur if schools concentrate on learning processes as articulated above.

Left and right brain thinking

How do we go about developing this reengineering mindset? Dent (1995) proposes that, in seeking to find ways of responding in a dynamic environment, we should examine left and right brain thinking. He distinguishes between them thus:

Table 2.2 Left and right brain functions (Dent 1995: 12)

Left brain	Right brain
• Repetitive	• Creative
• Systematic	• Complex
• Computational work	• Intuitive powers and judgement

He believes that the 'left brain' characteristics have served us adequately to date but that there is now a need for a greater emphasis on right brain thinking. He goes on to suggest that it is possible to use the concept of halves of the brain being very different to characterise incremental and radical innovators in the following ways:

Table 2.3 Incremental and radical innovators (Dent 1995: 269)

Incremental innovators	Radical innovators
Tend to:	Tend to:
• rely on the left brain	• rely on the right brain
• approach problems systematically	• approach problems from new angles
• be social and competitive	• be loners
• love results, progress and feedback	• love challenges and puzzles
• operate in neat methodical environments	• operate in messy environments
• be stable and measured	• be eccentric and moody
• be more serious	• have a strong sense of humour

Dent would see the encouragement of 'right brain' radical thinking as necessary to cope with the challenge of leading in the rapidly changing environment of the 21st century. In developing a futures perspective it is obviously important to encourage the right brain radical thinkers but also to enhance and encourage the capability of all individuals for radical thinking. It is valuable to consider the focus of staff development inset days over the last few years. In a period of increasing government imposed initiatives and change, schools often feel they are faced with 'innovation overload'. Responding to government initiatives such as the literacy and numeracy strategies, where the 'pack' is designed and delivered by government, teachers can often believe they are technicians delivering a centralised curriculum package.

The danger with this approach is that by its very nature it encourages left brain thinking where the creativity is at the design stage not at the implementation stage. The more that training days are devoted to external change initiatives, the less time there is for the staff to engage in right brain thinking to discuss how they work and learn, how children work and learn and how unique school-based solutions can be developed. Thus the challenge for the future for leaders in schools is to ensure that staff development activities provide enough time to support the development of right brain thinking in the school.

The Sigmoid curve

A useful tool to explore the need to rethink critically future direction is provided by Charles Handy (1994), who makes use of the Sigmoid curve.

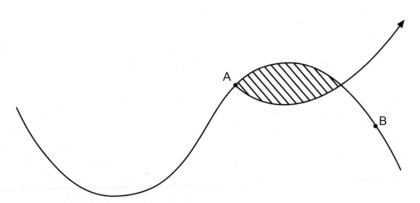

Figure 2.3 The Sigmoid curve (Handy 1994: 51)

Handy suggests that most organisations rise and fall or expand and contract in a way very similar to a sine wave. The challenge for leadership is to assess where the organisation is on the Sigmoid curve. As schools start to improve and move up the curve to point A, there is a danger that all the signals coming into the organisation say the school is doing well and it should keep on doing what it is already doing. Therein lies the danger. It is at point A that the school has the positive success culture and needs to rethink what it will mean to be successful in five years' time. What is the rethinking that needs to take place (the shaded area) so that the school reengineers how it operates and moves onto the next curve to become successful in the future environment in which it will be operating? If change does not take place, although increasingly successful in the short term, the school will eventually become less effective in the long term and decline to point B where achievement, morale and resources are in decline and change is difficult to effect. This analysis is also useful when applied to component parts within the school. For example, what does it mean to have an effective approach to science in the future? What does the science co-ordinator or head of science need to be aware of in current trends and possible future trends so that a dialogue and understanding can be built for greater effectiveness in the future?

Building an agenda for a futures dialogue and perspective in your school

Since 1989, there has been considerable government intervention in school improvement. It is clear, in England and Wales, that the initial purposes of a national curriculum have been achieved. Compared with the 1980s, there is a more consistent coverage of subjects in primary schools and pupils in secondary schools are required to follow a broader curriculum to the age of 16 (although, at the time of writing, this is under review). The aim of 'raising standards' has also been achieved through the linking of testing to the curriculum framework and, more importantly, through a focus on improvement at the classroom level. The dilemma of any national curriculum, however, is the one of setting up frameworks while, at the same time, providing flexibility and encouraging individual flair and responsiveness.

We believe that there are several aspects of education which will need fundamental rethinking at the school level for success in the future, now that the first waves of reform are in place. To what extent do different pupils need different curricula and different approaches to learning? Who will lead and manage this learning, what skills and competencies will they need and how will they be rewarded? Where and when will this learning take place? How will it be funded? What are the dilemmas around ensuring equity in a more differentiated learning environment? The answers to many of these questions will relate to the potential flexibilities (for a curriculum, for staffing and for resource use) around a common core.

Critics of futures thinking tend to rely on assertions that precise and detailed planning is not possible. That is certainly true but what is possible is to build a futures perspective in the school. This allows the school to build capability to understand trends and developments, to scan the environment and, most importantly, to build understanding of the nature of the trends as they develop.

Focusing on basic questions such as 'Why do we do what we do?', 'Does what we do contribute significant "added value" to the educational product?' and 'What do learners really need?' can be very valuable and can start the futures dialogue. The standard approach which asks 'Where are we now? Where do we want to get to?' is flawed because it encourages incremental movement forward. It is more effective to engage in 'planning backwards' by answering two basic questions:

- What sort of educational experience will learners have over the next seven to ten years and beyond?
- How will we plan to operate in this environment?

We now look at practical ways of initiating discussion on futures issues in a school.

Governors and senior team futures thinking

In order to create a futures dialogue, the governors and senior leadership team of a school need to separate out futures and strategic planning from operational issues (for an example, see Wise 2003 and page 106 of this book). The leadership team, working with governors, needs to create specific opportunities to share insights and broader perceptions about the future direction of the school. This can be in the formal meeting structure where longer-term review and planning take place as well as through an informal 'working dinner' where, once a term, there can be 'blue sky' thinking. In particular, it is important that key issues are identified and that the analysis then progresses through data collection to building intent. In some areas, some headteachers meet with other heads on a termly basis for this purpose, thus broadening the debate. National and international networks are also significant here.

Setting up a futures group in a school

This can consist of a group of people who meet at approximately two-monthly intervals to consider the impact of possible futures on the school. This group can take a number of forms but it may be most appropriate to have a cross-section of staff. Whatever grouping is chosen, it is important that the activity does not become a simple 'talking shop' but that some structure and coherence should be attempted.

This can be achieved in either of two ways as shown in the exercises below.

Exercise: Futures schematic

In this approach, the group starts with a 'clean slate' and engages in brainstorming, having an unstructured discussion which then can be formalised, perhaps using the framework shown in Table 2.4. When considering futures thinking it is important to look not just at the school sector but at the wider economic and social trends and to be creative by looking at a range of organisations and policies such as the information technology industry, the impact of the emerging economies, political and societal changes and their impact on the nature of work. The possible broader impact on the education sector can then be assessed.

> Undertake this brainstorming activity and then use the framework in Table 2.4 to record the outcomes of your discussions.

Table 2.4 Futures schematic framework

Area for consideration	Evidence of trends/directions	Possible implications for education

Exercise: Futures trends

A more structured approach would be to start with some predetermined futures list. We suggest that schools take our eleven points (discussed earlier in this chapter) as a start and, after discussion, identify five areas which they wish to monitor. Then, two or three times a year, they can undertake to report any significant developments or any items that need adding to the list of five.

Choose five of the changes outlined on pages 10 to 26 which your school should examine over the next 12 to 24 months. The aim should be to build in staff and governors the capability to understand the implications of these trends for the school. Choose those about which you, as a group, have little awareness, have not looked at recently or which might be particularly significant for your school. The focusing should allow the school to use its time effectively. Consider the possible impact on the school of each of these and then suggest how the school might respond in order to cope with that impact, using the framework in Table 2.5.

Table 2.5 Futures trends framework

Area chosen	Potential impact on the school	School response
1.		
2.		
3.		
4.		
5.		

This chapter has sought to build a futures perspective and to emphasise the need for those in the school to engage in this long-term scanning. In the more intermediate future, strategy, strategic intent and strategic planning need to be employed. These concepts will be explored in the next chapter.

Chapter 3

Strategy
Strategic intent and strategic planning

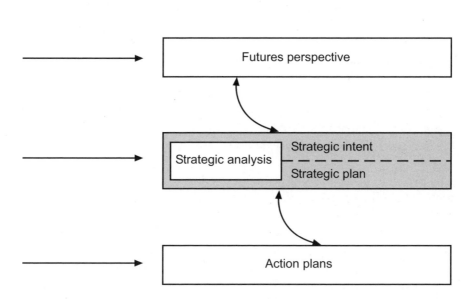

Introduction

We hope that Chapter Two has given school leaders the impetus and ideas to engage in a futures dialogue and to build a futures perspective. Once this outward and forward-looking mindset has been established, it will be necessary to seek ways in which the school might prepare both the school and the pupils for the future. This requires that the school develops a strategy which, in our terminology, deals with the medium-term, i.e. three to five years into the future so that we very often talk about strategy as taking us to 'where we want to be in five years' time'.

Before examining approaches to developing strategies, it is important to define some of the characteristics of strategy that we use in this book:

1. Strategy deals with the *medium- to longer-term* (three to five years).
2. Strategy deals with *fundamental or important key issues*. It concentrates on the overall direction and the major themes of the organisation. It does not replicate all the items of the traditional school development plan but, instead, it draws together key themes.
3. Strategy deals with *broad aggregated data*. It does not replicate the detail of short-term planning. For example, if a school has 300 pupils, for strategic planning purposes it does not matter if, in five years' time, the school has 280 or 320 students as, in broad terms, it will be the same size of school. It does, of course, matter in the short-term if an extra 20 pupils turn up next term! This latter is the short-term imperative, compared with the longer-term perspective and is dealt with through the action plan. Adding an extra year of detail to an existing three-year school development plan does not make it strategic!
4. Strategy should be seen as a *template* against which to benchmark current activity. Thus if requests for current expenditure come across a headteacher's desk they should be checked to see if they are contributing to strategic goals.

The problem of developing strategy in education is that there is often a feeling of being unable to control, at the school level, what is happening because of externally imposed changes but this is, perhaps, an inappropriate excuse for not developing relevant strategies for the school. Some schools already have a strategic plan in order to realise their intended strategy. They see this plan as a rational proposal that rolls out over a three- to five-year period. Other schools have not gone down this route, believing that the pace of change is so great and so unpredictable that such plans are overtaken; these schools simply create a new one- to two-year plan each year but do not have any discussion about the future of the school. We believe that some aspects of a school's activities are quite predictable or determinable while other aspects are less so but still need consideration. We try, in this chapter, to develop approaches to meet these two different requirements.

Establishing a conceptual framework for strategy development

In order to establish a strategy, it is important to understand the factors which determine the most appropriate approach to strategy development. We have found that Boisot (1995) provides a very valuable framework for analysing approaches to strategy development in relation to levels of environmental turbulence and of organisational and individual understanding. The framework is based on four perspectives of strategy: strategic planning, emergent strategy, intrapreneurship and strategic intent. In Figure 3.1 the vertical axis relates to the degree of educational and more general environmental change. Because change is often considered to be rational and linear, Boisot uses the term turbulence to signify a more dynamic and unpredictable type of change. The horizontal axis relates to the level of understanding that an individual or an organisation has of the turbulence and change in which it exists. Boisot articulates a model of strategy in which one of the four strategic responses or approaches is particularly appropriate to a specific combination of turbulence and understanding as follows.

Strategic planning is effective in an environment in which there is a low to medium rate of change and the school can understand, react to and cope with that change. While schools exist in a turbulent environment, there are aspects of their work which are more predictable. In such a situation the school can have a clear strategic plan for these definable parts of its activities. An example of a definable area would be pupil progression. Many schools should find it

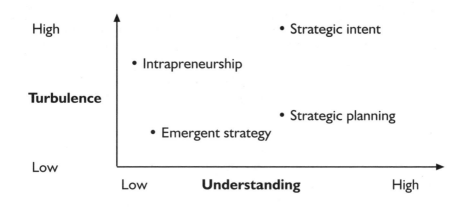

Figure 3.1 Typology of strategies (Boisot 1995: 40)

reasonably straightforward to plan that their five-year-olds become six-year-olds and then seven-year-olds and so on. So, estimating pupil numbers can have a degree of plannable predictability about it for these schools. There are, however, schools in which pupil turnover is very high and numbers change quite considerably so that this degree of predictability would not be possible and strategic planning would be less appropriate because of this turbulence. Another example would be the appointment of newly qualified teachers to the school as they will cause 'incremental drift' for the school's budget as they move up the incremental salary scale. This is predictable and can be planned for. Whatever happens to government initiatives, the centrality of core literacy and numeracy in the school's curriculum is likely to remain. In essence, strategic planning assumes that people know where they are going, that they know how to get there and the process is thus predicable and definable. It is, by its very nature, a proactive approach. Thus, in Figure 3.1, strategic planning fits into the bottom right-hand quadrant as it is appropriate when there is a high level of understanding and a low to medium rate of change or turbulence.

In the educational context, rapid change over the last ten years, both from government policy initiatives and from a number of factors (such as the changing economic, social and technological environment) impacting on learning has cast doubts as to whether strategic planning is possible for all of a school's activities. Schools have been encouraged to extend their development planning period from one or two years up to five years and have tried to make plans for this less predicable environment. Whether it is practicable to do this remains in some doubt. Boisot (1995) suggests that alternative approaches should be considered.

Emergent strategy can best be understood as a reactive approach. It is a process of learning by doing, through trial and error. When faced with adapting to, or coping with, low to medium levels of change, if there is a low level of understanding of that change, the best way to proceed is to attempt a number of activities and reflect on which have been successful and which have been less successful. By reflecting back on that experience, the school should repeat the successful activities and not repeat the unsuccessful ones. Thus by this reflecting back on past experience, a strategic path appears and it can be used for strategy formulation in the future. It is a little like walking through a minefield in the desert – if you cross it successfully it is possible to look back at the footprints in the sand and say that was the best path. It is not so clear-cut at the start of the journey!

This discovering of strategy by doing is often associated with incremental change whereby adjustments are made to the planned strategy as new information becomes available. Thus, the schools can respond and adjust as each new change 'hits' them. Schools, when faced with a series of new initiatives from central or local government, react and adjust to them and a strategy for dealing with them in the longer-term should emerge later.

Intrapreneurship assumes that there is a high degree of turbulence in the system and that the centre of the organisation does not have the understanding to plan in a detailed way. As a result, decentralised units are encouraged to plan according to their specific circumstances as long as they focus on two or three central directives. Thus, localised successes and failures build a direction for the organisation. For the education sector as a whole, the multiple initiatives of the late 1980s were imposed upon schools at the same time that they were given greater autonomy at the site level to manage their responses. As such, it could be considered that the national government had little understanding as to how the implementation would be accomplished, but merely held the sub-units (the LEAs or the schools) accountable by two or three central measures such as testing and OFSTED inspection. Similarly, the headteacher of a large secondary or primary school, faced with the then new national curriculum over the full range of subjects, could not hope individually to plan a detailed response in each area. With a high volume of change over such a range of subjects and the inability to understand the detail of each, the only sensible way forward was to let the individual curriculum leaders develop their own understandings and responses within central guidelines. Thus, intrapreneurship is an appropriate strategy in a given set of circumstances where a balance between central broad frameworks and local planning is desirable.

Strategic intent, the final approach, is one which has a great deal of value for the educationalist. Intent is about setting a series of achievable, but significantly challenging activities that 'leverage up' the organisation to perform at much higher levels in specific and definable areas. Thus, developing a 'success and high achievement culture' across the whole ability range instead of trying to raise pass rates by 2% or 3% for borderline children can be seen to be an example that delineates an intent from a specific plan. Another example would be developing a culture of independent technology-based learning in the school. Strategic intent is a very powerful way of linking futures thinking and strategy as a means of providing direction and purpose for an organisation whereas broad visions or goals may be too vague to be of practical use to the school. The concept of strategic intent will be explored in more detail below.

Utilising two key strategic approaches for schools

We believe that some aspects of a school's activities are quite predictable or determinable while other aspects are less so. In the sections which follow, we try to develop approaches to meet these two different requirements. We propose the concept of strategic intent which we believe is a more appropriate way of building capability and capacity in a school for the less predictable aspects of provision. We then discuss strategic planning as being appropriate for the 'determinable' aspects of medium-term planning. The word capacity is used to mean the extent to which an organisation has the total amount of resources to undertake an activity while the term capability indicates the extent to which the quality of those resources enables the activity to be completed successfully.

Developing strategic intent in schools

Strategic intent is described by Boisot (1995: 36) as 'a process of coping with turbulence through a direct, intuitive understanding, emanating from the top of the firm *(i.e. organisation)* and guiding its efforts'. We would suggest that a school which is dealing with either a longer-term time frame or a less predictable environment needs to build in all of its staff a common strategic intent, based on the values and ambitions of the school, which all staff can articulate and to which they can align themselves. Thus, faced with new and untried situations they can draw on that common understanding as a frame of reference.

Davies (2002b) articulates a model of developing strategic intent as shown in Figure 3.2.

The ABCD model articulates a process whereby leaders in an organisation articulate a sense of direction by drawing together their knowledge of the internal nature of the school with the external influences to identify areas in which the school needs to build capability and capacity to move forward. To create this awareness and sense of direction, the leader develops understanding by sharing images and experiences and using metaphors to build a picture of what an

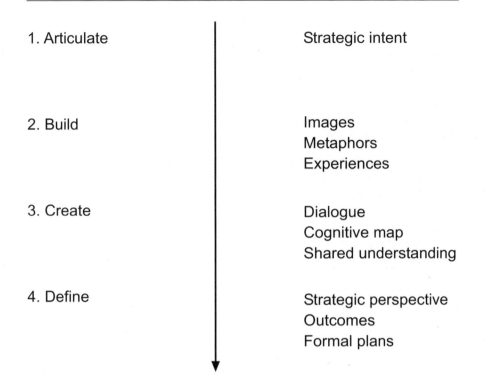

1. Articulate	Strategic intent
2. Build	Images Metaphors Experiences
3. Create	Dialogue Cognitive map Shared understanding
4. Define	Strategic perspective Outcomes Formal plans

Figure 3.2 The ABCD model of building strategic intent (Davies 2002b: 204)

alternative direction or state of the school could be. Once this picture is established, then a dialogue and a strategic conversation can take place between all those working in the organisation. This dialogue establishes a mental or cognitive map leading to a shared understanding amongst those working in the school. Only then is it possible to move to establishing a strategic perspective and defining outcomes and formal plans.

This contrasts with strategic planning which immediately goes straight to Stage 4, 'define'. Strategic intent allows the building of meaning and purpose but also allows time to establish capability and capacity to tackle the challenge. As such it allows leaders to say they know where they are going but they don't know how to get there yet! Eventually when they do, by building capability and capacity, strategic intents will change into more formal strategic plans. In order to demonstrate what we mean by strategic intent, we now show strategic intents for a school.

Example: Brentwich School

Brentwich School, after undertaking a 'futures awareness' training session and an extensive strategic analysis, decided to focus on building capability and capacity to deal with five key intents identified by the leadership and staff (see Table 3.1).

Table 3.1 Strategic intents for Brentwich School

Strategic intents for the school
1. Create a high expectation and success culture
2. Design and implement accurate performance indicators and hold everyone accountable for them
3. Establish technology-based individual learning for all pupils
4. Build 'leadership in depth' throughout the staff
5. Link home and school through the development of a learning community

These challenging intents are seen as a framework and capability-building agenda for the school to work through. The outcome in detailed terms and the means of achieving it will be worked out during the three- to five-year time-frame. Table 3.2 shows how the school will then break down each of the intents into a set of activities through which it will build the capability to work towards achieving that intent. At the end of the specified period, there will be a number of possible outcomes:

- The capability will have been developed and any further activities will be moved into the action plan.
- Some capability will have been developed but definable medium-term developments are still required so those will be built into the strategic plan.
- Capability will need further development through the strategic intent process.

Table 3.2 Building capability towards strategic intent

Intent	Capability-building measures	Outcomes
1.Create a high expect-ation and success culture	i. Celebrate success ii. Communicate targets iii. No failure culture iv. Find something for each child to succeed at v. Staff training to ensure the school reinforces the positive vi. Focus success on teams	• The capability will have been developed and any further activities will be moved into the action plans
2.Design and implement accurate performance indicators and hold everyone accountable for them	i. Staff development on target-setting ii. Create individual pupil, staff and organisational targets for day-to-day use iii. Create information system to provide accurate assessments on demand iv. Create self-reviewing teams v. Build into performance management system vi. Investigate resources to support	• Some capability will have been developed but definable medium-term developments are still required so those will be built into the strategic plan
3.Establish technology-based individual learning for all pupils	i. Scan environment for latest developments in technology ii. Investigate devoting more curriculum time to study skills and independent learning skills for pupils iii. Create a culture where all staff are IT literate and integrate it into their teaching iv. Investigate potential sponsorship and resource support	

continued ...

Table 3.2 continued

Intent	Capability-building measures	Outcomes
4.Build 'leadership in depth' throughout the staff	i. Support staff to take on responsibility to deal with issues as they arise ii. Provide leadership and management develop-ment for all staff iii. Develop a 'no blame culture' where staff are encouraged to take risks iv. Provide a forum for staff to discuss their roles in an ever-changing environment	↕
5.Link home and school through the develop-ment of a learning community	i. Set up discussion forum with community to consider the nature of potential links ii. Evaluate how open access, Internet, the Learning Grid and other technology creates a learning centre for the whole community all day and all year iii. Investigate resources, possible funds, bidding strategies iv. Create an Open Door culture	• Capability will need further development through the strategic intent process

Strategic planning

We now focus on one specific aspect of strategy development and a process which schools are being encouraged to use to create three- or five-year plans, that of strategic planning for an intended course of action. Strategic planning is useful for the more predictable and controllable elements within the planning processes, especially when these are incremental and linear and where a good understanding of the detail is possible. In our definition earlier we suggested that:

(i)   strategy deals with the medium- to longer-term,
(ii) strategy deals with fundamental or important key issues,
(iii) strategy deals with broad aggregated data,
(iv) strategy should be seen as a template against which to benchmark current activity.

Strategic planning involves journey thinking in which we are extrapolating patterns from the past and projecting to the future. It takes the broader organisational view. By articulating the main features of the organisation's development, it projects forward several years. As such it can be considered to be a rational, predictable and, to a large degree, an incremental process.

What would a strategic plan look like in a school? We suggest it would have a number of key features. Instead of being the traditional school development plan 'list of tasks to be done', it would aggregate these numerous activities into a limited number of strategic areas. The examples in Tables 3.3 and 3.4 show how the core purpose of the school, the *learning outcomes* is the first strategic planning area followed by *the support for the quality of the learning and teaching processes* to achieve this. The third area comprises a number of *leadership and management arrangements* which underpin the activities above and, finally, there are *the resource and structural issues* which support the school's development. The strategic planning activities that are undertaken are definable and achievable within a given time frame and the people responsible for achieving and monitoring the activities are listed, together with associated costs. In the case studies in Chapters Six to Eight, we will show how this has been adapted in a primary school, a secondary school and an LEA. The important factor in this process is for the leader in the school to focus on aggregated strategic data and activities and not to become involved in the detail of the action planning process.

Table 3.3 Primary case example – Strategic Plan 2002 to 2007

Strategic planning area	Strategic planning activities	Time frame 3–5 Years	Costs	Responsibility	Monitoring	Evaluation
Learning outcomes: pupil progress & achievement	1. Improve standards in basic literacy: no more than 5% pupils with reading age below chronological age, at least 35% achieving Level 5 English.	3 years	This will vary according to the size of school – include both material and staff development costs	English SL	Governor	SLT
	2. Raise standards of numeracy: 85% achieving at least NC level for age.	4 years		Maths SL	Governor	SLT
	3. All pupils engaged in independent technology-based learning	3 years		ICT SL	Governor	SLT
	4. Include more curriculum time on the creative and expressive arts.	4 years		SL Art & Mus	Governor	KSC
Support for the quality of learning & teaching processes	1. Quality of teaching – refocus professional development.	3 years		Deputy	Governor	SLT
	2. Reconceptualise the learning day to integrate the role of the home and community.	5 years		Community liaison	Governor	SLT
	3. Develop a whole-school approach to science.	3 years		Science SL	Governor	SLT
Leadership & management arrangements	1. Develop leadership in depth.	4 years		Deputy	Governor	SLT
	2. Integrate performance management process to link to SIP and professional learning process.	4 years		Headteacher	Governor	Staffing sub com
	3. Increase Governors' involvement with monitoring and evaluation.	3 years		Headteacher	Governor	Gov bod
Physical & financial resources, school structure & organisation	1. Technology equipment – increase level of provision.	3 years		ICT SL	Governor	SLT
	2. Rewiring and refurbishment of key areas.	4 years		Buildings subcommittee	Head	SLT
	3. Building extension – raise funds and start.	3 years		Buildings subcommittee	Head	SLT

Table 3.4 Secondary case example – Strategic Plan 2002 to 2007

Strategic planning area	Strategic planning activities	Time frame 3–5 Years	Costs	Responsibility	Monitoring	Evaluation
Learning outcomes: pupil progress & achievement	1. Improve levels of literacy in Key Stage 3 – 74% pupils to reach Level 5 by end of Year 9: 36% to reach Level 6. 2. Raise standards of numeracy in Key Stage 4, all pupils to achieve a grade at GCSE; 60% to reach C or above. 3. All pupils involved in independent technology-based learning beyond the traditional classroom	3 years 4 years 3 years	This will vary according to the size of school – include both material and staff development costs	HOD/English HOD/Maths ICT co-ord	DHI DHI DH2	Head/Gov Head/Gov Head/Gov
Support for the quality of learning & teaching processes	1. Develop staff capability for more technology-based learning: using electronic whiteboards, laptops for teaching and learning etc. 2. Widen the provision for able children across all subjects, both within and beyond the normal lessons. 3. Introduce a more relenze approach to the curriculum for the lower ability pupils in Key Stage 4.	3 years 4 years 3 years		ICT co-ord & DH2 HOD/HOY KS4 co-ord	DHI DHI Ast Head	Head/Gov Head/Gov DHI
Leadership & management arrangements	1. Improve quality of teaching in relation to OFSTED criteria. 2. Develop leadership in depth within the school. 3. Ensure that all staff are skilled in using value-added data and target-setting to raise achievement and are supported by an efficient and accessible information system.	4 years 4 years 3 years		HODs/DH2 DH2 HOD/Ast Head	Head Head DHI	Head/Gov Head/DHI Head
Physical & financial resources, school structure & organisation	1. Increase level of computer provision by 100 machines. 2. Rewiring and refurbishment of lower school building (including ISDN links). 3. Building extension – commission estimates, raise funds and start new 6th Form Centre.	3 years 5 years 3 years		ICT co-ord Bursar Premises–Gov	Ast Head DH2 Chair Gov	DH2 Governors Governors

In our experience, many people in a wide range of schools have found this to be a format which is easy to understand and which is systematic. It has the benefit of focusing activities around a set of major strategic activities and, by so doing, provides a clear agenda for the school. In the next chapter we look at strategic analysis. Planning is an iterative process and there is not a definitive starting point as schools are working from their current situation. Either a school can start with the analysis and write the plan or can have a planning framework and undertake the analysis to develop different courses of action within the plan. In practice schools will work concurrently on both. In sequencing the chapters we have put analysis next but it could have come before this chapter – it is a matter of personal preference.

Chapter 4

Strategic analysis
Gathering and interpreting the information

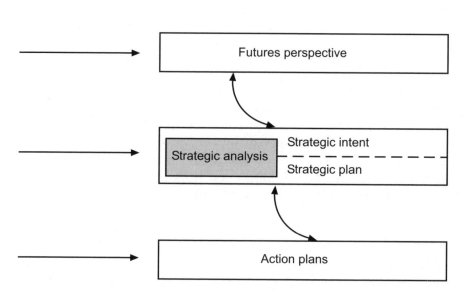

Introduction

Strategic analysis aims to form a view of the key factors which will influence the school in the medium term. These factors will affect the strategies which are chosen to achieve the strategic intent and the strategic plan. The process of strategic analysis can be seen in practical terms to involve three sequential processes: first, obtaining strategic data from a variety of sources; second, analysing, interpreting and integrating these data to turn them into useful information; third, even if a desirable option is indicated, checking as to whether the organisation's context and culture make that option feasible. This process will result in an aggregated strategic view of the school in order to inform the planning process.

Our research for the second edition of this book has yielded many valuable insights from leading practitioners in schools. One of these insights is that schools which can sustain improvement over a period of time not only have plans which are strategic but they engage in the art of strategic conversation. It is as important to build a dialogue around strategy and a perspective of strategy as it is to have actual strategic plans. If a strategy is to work, the intellectual resources of the organisation must contribute to the interpretation of the data and, in doing so, gain ownership and be able to be committed to the strategic direction which the school chooses. A view sometimes articulated of 'middle managers' is that they do not have a broad strategic view, only a narrow and operational one. They will only achieve this broad view if they are engaged in a strategic dialogue within their school, for example through involvement with senior staff in whole-school issues. If this dialogue is to be worthwhile, adequate time needs to be set aside for it. It is not very effective to work through a long agenda of detailed actions and activities and then, towards the end of a meeting to suggest that the participants engage in a broad debate about significant areas of development for the school over the medium- to longer-term. A better approach is to separate out operational and strategic items and have separate meetings for each. Figure 3.2 on page 41 regarding building strategic intent is important here. The second and third stages, 'building' and 'creating', especially the strategic dialogue or conversation, are critical in defining strategy and proceeding towards the formal plans. Any dialogue about the future of the school needs to be based on information created from a wide range of data, some of which are broad and some of which are focused and more detailed.

In the sections which follow, we discuss the types of broad and more focused and detailed data and the ways in which they can be gathered.

A broad strategic analysis

Although the data on the broad strategic environment will usually be assembled by the senior leadership team, to appreciate fully the strategic position of the school it is necessary to understand how a wide range of stakeholders, such as pupils, staff, employers, governors and the community, view the situation which the school faces and its possible direction. Those responsible for aspects of the analysis need to look beyond their normal sources of information if the work is to have validity. This is the basis of the strategic conversation with stakeholders.

One of the most significant strategic roles for school leadership is 'scanning the horizon', that is seeing beyond the boundaries of the school and understanding the interface between the school and its environment. We consider that obtaining a broad strategic analysis consists of a *STEEP* learning curve! This involves the stakeholders in scanning or reviewing the following aspects of the strategic environment:

Social environment
Technological environment
Educational environment
Economic environment
Political environment

Those who engage constantly in futures thinking should be very aware of the broad trends in each of the five environmental areas. Here we seek to remind readers to consider those trends and thus to bring their implications into the broad planning process. We seek also to encourage schools to look to international comparisons and trends as well as national and regional information.

Understanding the 'broad backcloth' of the five aspects of the environment enables educational leaders to reflect on the context in which the more focused strategic analysis is taking place. We list below some of the questions which schools should seek to answer as they analyse the broader environment.

Social environment

- How is society changing and how is this affecting the local community, for example in terms of cultural mix, demography, family patterns?
- How are patterns of work and leisure changing in the community?
- What is the school's role in promoting the development of social capital?

Technological environment

- What are the changes in the nature, availability and capability of technology?
- How do changes in learning and teaching technologies affect the nature and location of learning and teaching?
- How do developments in technology alter the nature and location of work?

Educational environment

- How much central government control and intervention is there and how does that affect school development?
- What are the accountability frameworks and how do these affect parental choice, for example through providing measures of output and value-added?
- What are the expectations about the learning process, for example a focus on the importance of the individual learner in relation to pace and preferred style of learning?
- What is the relevance of the boundaries between different stages of education and between education and the community?
- In what ways do society and the local community have changing and conflicting views of the purpose of education and of schooling?
- How are the leadership and management functions in schools changing?

Economic environment

- How are the changing patterns of industry and commerce, for example increasing moves in employment from the manufacturing to the services sector, affecting education, in particular at 14–19?
- What are the trends in relating value-added educational gains to resource levels, so that schools can be compared in terms of 'value for money' with the drive to achieve increased performance with the same resource level?
- How are patterns of working affecting staffing and professional development in schools, for example portfolio careers in which adults hold several jobs at once and change career several times?
- What are the potential staff recruitment and retention difficulties and what are the potential associated increased costs for schools?
- What might be the potential changes in staffing patterns and arrangements, such as more para-professionals, core and periphery staff, fixed-term performance-led contracts, site-based pay bargaining?
- What is the effect of greater varieties of finance with blurring between state-only and private-only funding of public services, including education?
- What are the implications of the government control of spending through specific grants?

Political environment

- What changes are being brought about by regionalisation of public sector provision?
- What is the effect of significantly enhanced levels of consumer choice, for example on differentiation between schools and the parents' choices?
- How is the government's tendency to micro-manage the public sector impacting at the school level?
- What is the impact of the contracting-out of educational as well as service elements of schooling?
- What is the impact at the school level of changes to the management of local services, for example privatisation of LEA functions?

To provide a structure for schools to engage in this broad strategic analysis, a strategic group in the school may wish to engage initially in a strategic conversation and, as that conversation develops, use a version of the matrix given in Table 4.1 to record in each of the categories below the significant changes that the participants consider will affect the school.

Table 4.1 STEEP analysis at various levels

	International	National	Local
Social			
Technological			
Educational			
Economic			
Political			

A focused strategic analysis

As well as analysing the broad trends, a school will need more detailed information in order to make planning decisions. We have found the following three headings useful as a way of grouping this more focused information and each of these will be explored in the text which follows.

- Analysing the school's stakeholders
- Analysing the school's product and service
- Analysing the competitors

Analysing the school's stakeholders

Here the purpose is to identify two main sets of strategic information:

- who are the stakeholders, present and future?
- what are the stakeholders' wants and needs?

There are several caveats to offer to those who may consider these approaches. Vast amounts of data may be gathered with considerable time implications. It is better to think carefully about the type of information which the school requires before asking a lot of people a lot of questions. Also, the responses, particularly to attitude surveys, can be very disturbing. There needs to be careful preparation in relation to planning the dissemination of results. It is unwise to gather data and then to take no action on issues that arise, although the action needed may simply be to improve communication.

Who are the stakeholders, present and future?

Stakeholders can be divided into more homogeneous groups in order to identify particular wants, needs and influencing factors. Appropriate products and services can then be developed and effective means of communication can be devised. A first step could be to divide the stakeholders into those internal and those external to the school, as shown in Table 4.2. Within these categories, there are various sub-divisions, for example of pupils according to age, staff according to experience or function, governors according to areas of interest or influence and visitors according to affiliation and purpose. Once the groupings have been identified, the school can then move on to examine a range of information such as numbers, gender, location and so on.

Table 4.2 Internal and external stakeholders of the school

Internal stakeholders	External stakeholders
• Governors	• Prospective students
• Staff (teaching and support)	• Prospective staff
• Regular visitors and helpers	• Former students
• Current students	• Other educational institutions
	• The local community
	• Commerce & industry
	• LEA
	• OFSTED
	• TTA/GTC/NCSL
	• DfES
	• National groups/organisations

What are the stakeholders' wants and needs?

In countries which offer parents and pupils a choice of schools, the very survival of the school depends on taking account of their values and preferences (or wants). An awareness of need allows the school to develop appropriate activities and then to target those most likely to benefit. It avoids the school falling into the trap of 'producer capture' in which the deliverers determine the product without reference to the consumers. It is, however, important for educational leaders to avoid the reactive approach in which an over-emphasis is given to a wide spectrum of consumer demands so that the educational needs of children are not being met. Some customers/clients express wants strongly and may falsely influence the view of needs. If school leaders are fully informed about clients' preferences, they are then able to adjust provision if it is inappropriate or to communicate more effectively the existing provision.

• When examining *parental* wants there should be an examination of current wants and future possible wants or preferences. This can be achieved by using interviews, focus groups or questionnaires or by using secondary data available locally or from national statistics and research projects (see page 62).

The core business of the school is to meet the needs of the *pupils* so it is important to identify these clearly. The school must ensure that it has efficient ways of gathering the range of data in Table 4.3, much of which will come from school records.

Table 4.3 Data requirements for the school

- The socio-cultural background of the pupils
- Pupil potential
- Levels of attainment and learning difficulties prior to entry
- Appropriate learning strategies
- Achievement and attainment throughout the time that a pupil is in school
- National educational requirements, e.g. relating to curriculum and assessment
- The future needs of the current pupils (e.g. through an understanding of environmental factors)
- The needs of future pupils

In order to ensure that the school develops the capability to meet the pupil needs, there must be an analysis of the developmental requirements (for knowledge, skills and understanding) of the other internal clients such as the staff and governors.

Analysing the school's product and service

The product and service of a school needs to be analysed in its broadest sense. While much of the professional focus will be on the curriculum and assessment, those outside the school may make their judgements based on the effectiveness of communications, pupil behaviour and the possession by the pupils of basic and social skills. In planning an analysis of its product and service, all aspects of the school should be listed, especially bearing in mind those areas which the clients feel are its significant activities. This list would include the items shown in Table 4.4.

Various tools and techniques are available to analyse the situation in each area, some of which are explained on pages 60–3. The suitability of each will depend on a range of factors such as the time available,

Table 4.4 The school's product and service

- The formal curriculum
- Learning and teaching strategies used (in terms of range and effectiveness)
- Measures of literacy, numeracy and cognitive ability
- Assessment and testing processes
- Ability and attainment levels on entry and exit
- Provision for special educational needs
- External test/examination results at the various age stages
- Calculations of value added – over time, by individuals, teachers and pupils, by teams and in proportion to resources
- Extra-curricular activities
- Pupil discipline and appearance
- Relationships
- Resources levels and utilisation of resources – time, materials, hardware
- Staff skills and abilities in terms of learning and teaching skills and experience
- Perceptions of the pupil experience from the customer viewpoint
- Environment
- Ethos

the people to be involved and the culture of the organisation. In addition to these, a SWOT analysis is a commonly used tool that provides an analysis of the strengths and weaknesses of the school, the opportunities which are available and the threats which it faces, as perceived by a range of stakeholders. This is a quick and easy means of gathering information although it must be interpreted with care. The process is more fully developed in our book on strategic marketing (Davies and Ellison 1997b). We also use the technique later in this chapter as a means of collating and interpreting data.

Analysing the competitors

The information gathered about the competitive forces acting on the school can be very significant in determining an appropriate strategic direction. There are considerable issues here because of parental choice, developments in the learning technology and changes in the funding of education and in the continuum of education itself.

Using concepts developed by Porter (1980) and Bowman and Asch (1987), we have developed the framework in Figure 4.1 to show the forces acting upon a school. We believe that the existing and potential new providers of education impact on a school as do the users of the school and the suppliers of services to the school. It is important to analyse the nature of these forces and power relationships in order to be proactive in planning the school's strategic response.

Each of the four areas will now be discussed.

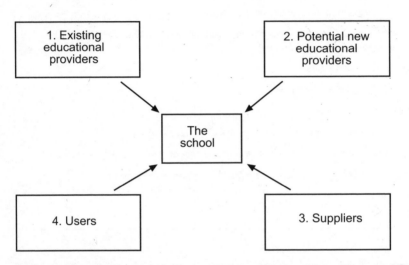

Figure 4.1 Strategic forces impacting on the school (adapted from Davies and Ellison 1997b: 59)

1.   Existing educational providers

It is important to analyse other schools, as benchmarking against schools in a regional or wider national or even international setting can provide a broader perception of what can be achieved. It is also important to analyse schools that are in the immediate environment as they exert power in the form of alternatives through the parental choice mechanism. Schools need to look beyond the immediate area as the development of specialist schools means that these schools draw from a wider catchment area. Good sources of information about other providers are: governors, parents, those who have chosen other schools, newspaper features, prospectuses, OFSTED reports and league tables.

2. *Potential new educational providers*

In a rapidly changing environment, schools as learning organisations are increasingly under pressure as alternatives emerge from which pupils and their parents may choose. Some alternatives are new schools or developments of existing schools such as the move to faith based schools or City Academies. Others are more radical such as home schooling which becomes more feasible as information technology becomes more sophisticated and able to provide curriculum programmes, learning resources, links to other organisations and so on.

Schools need to consider whether they can turn these perceived threats into opportunities by integrating the ideas into their own provision or whether they should compete based on other strengths. There is a need to think creatively and to look beyond education for trends which can be ascertained from the broader changes in the economy and technology.

3. *Suppliers*

Suppliers of goods or labour to the school can exert a powerful force so it is important to bear them in mind during strategic analysis. It may be that most of the factors are included elsewhere in the analysis but the following checklists need to be considered.

Suppliers of goods and services:

- Which are the main suppliers?
- Are the suppliers likely to be available in the future?
- What are the pricing and service level trends in each case?
- Is the school likely to be tied to the suppliers in any way, e.g. because of sponsorship deals, monopolies or legal requirements?

Suppliers of labour:

- Is there an adequate and appropriate supply from which to choose or should the school seek to improve the supply?
- How stable is the current labour supply?
- How much flexibility is there in the current labour supply?
- What are the cost implications of the current labour supply?

In an era of teacher shortage and with a limited availability of supply teachers, labour costs will be 'bid up' over the next few years.

Analysis of the situation will allow the school to make appropriate plans or develop strategic intent (for example, to 'grow' their own teachers through school-based routes) to ensure that cost-effective supplies of goods and labour are available and that the school is not driven by such powers.

4.   Users

A school is mainly funded on a 'per capita' basis so that an appropriate number of 'users' in the form of pupils or other funded learners is critical to its ability to remain cost-effective and 'in business'. Depending on the age of the pupils, it may be that the actual choice decision is significantly influenced by the parents. The factors which influence choice will have been considered in the section on stakeholder wants above. It might be useful to consider here the nature of the power which the users hold. If, for example, there are several ways of obtaining a similar type of education, then it is easy for users to change and they are quite powerful. Thus, issues such as a differentiated curriculum and a lack of geographical competitors weaken the power of the user. Conversely, a national curriculum, an effective transport system (or parents to act as 'chauffeurs') or a technology-based alternative strengthen the power of the user.

The users of the output of education, i.e. other schools, the community and employers, exert power on schools. It is important to analyse their requirements in order to inform strategic developments.

How to undertake the data collection

Collecting accurate data is critical for good strategic decision-making. The danger is that those in the school leadership team make assumptions based on past experience and do not check against current reality by undertaking to collect current data. Some of the means of gathering data are listed below and then explained in more detail.

1. Interviews and focus groups
2. Questionnaires and attitude surveys
3. Monitoring, evaluation and inspection reports
4. Secondary data available locally or from national statistics and research projects

1. Interviews and focus groups

Focus groups occur when a group of stakeholders (say eight or ten) are invited to discuss current education or plans for the future of that education or the direction of the school. The advantage of this is that not only can an initial variety of views be obtained but the process of articulation in a group situation triggers off a rich diversity of views and information which can contribute to a wealth of data.

One way of collecting data is to interview a group of parents. This could be done when they come to a parents' evening (although this may not be representative). Another way is to select a cross section of parents in a particular year group and undertake telephone interviews with them in the evening to elicit their views on their child's experience of education in the school.

2. Questionnaires and attitude surveys

These will enable the school to assess the perceptions which the existing and potential customers have of education in general and of the school in particular. If information gathered is to be valid, school leaders must give serious thought to the data collection process and to anonymity. We have been involved in several research projects in this area, including working with schools to investigate the perceptions of a large number of pupils, their parents and the staff.

We feel that it is important to strike a cautionary note about the need to find out what the clients *really* think, rather than to make assumptions about their perceptions of the school's product and service. Also, these perceptions may not reflect the reality in the school but be the result of poor communication. Further investigation may be needed and a range of clients should be considered because different clients and client groups will have a different perception of the same aspect of provision.

3. Monitoring, evaluation and inspection reports

i) Internal monitoring and evaluation

These processes would take place as part of the school's normal management cycle and would provide an ongoing source of information for the planning process. There is now a considerable emphasis on school self-evaluation.

ii)   External monitoring, evaluation and inspection

All maintained schools in England and Wales are inspected by OFSTED (England) or ESTYN (Wales) so that the publicly available reports can give an insight about a particular school, but it is also possible to glean useful information from the reports of other schools and from the published summaries of overall findings. In addition, LEA reviews and those of subject experts and consultants give useful data.

Performance and assessment data (PANDA) reports are provided by the DfES. Each PANDA report contains basic information about a school, i.e. the context in which it works, a summary of key performance data broken down by key stages and comparison with similar schools. Accompanying the PANDA report is an annex called the National Summary Data Report (NSDR). The NSDR contains guidance and an extensive range of information collated from inspection evidence allowing comparisons such as pupil–teacher ratios, unit costs, and patterns of strengths and weaknesses in schools nationally.

4.   Secondary data available locally or from national statistics and research projects

Educational researchers provide a wealth of information. The research by Glatter, Woods and Bagley (1995) which covered a range of types of school, socio-economic circumstances and area, demonstrated that parents have common priorities when choosing schools:

- Child's preference for the school
- Standard of academic education
- Nearness to home/convenience for travel
- Child's happiness at the school.

A very perceptive review of the field was produced by Gorard (1999) which is a summary of research produced on school choice and is recommended for detailed study. He outlines the following as criteria for choice used by parents:

- Safety and welfare of pupil (includes well-behaved pupils and no bullying)
- Academic outcomes (examination results and good teaching)
- School resources (range of subjects and quality of classrooms)

- Traditional style
- Small school/class
- Extra-curricular activities.

How to analyse data and build an aggregated strategic view of the school

Once all the information has been gathered together, it needs to be organised in some useful way in order to inform the choice of direction for the school. We would suggest that if school leaders tell their staff that they are going to use the OFSTED framework, it would not necessarily fill their hearts with joy! There are many ways in which this *integration* of information can be achieved. What is needed is something to achieve a paradigm shift to allow people to think differently. We describe below the use of three tools or models which we have chosen because they have allowed this different perspective to be developed and have proved very useful to a variety of school leaders with whom we have worked. Schools, especially large ones, will acquire a large amount of information as a result of the processes described above. Senior staff will then need to find ways to put the information together to build up a coherent picture of the school's position. We have found it valuable to use the following tools for analysis as a means of using some of the detailed information gathered to form this more focused view.

1. Boston Consulting Group (BCG) matrix
2. Comparative stakeholder analysis
3. SWOT analysis

In addition, we suggest a feasibility assessment, the Feasibility and Desirability Matrix, which can be used when considering possible developments.

1. Boston Consulting Group (BCG) matrix

The BCG matrix was devised for the analysis of strategic positioning and strategic development in business units within large companies, so we have adapted it for an educational setting. The matrix is divided into four quadrants as shown in Figure 4.2.

The purpose of the matrix is to position items that have emerged from the data collection on the matrix. It is important to limit this to

Figure 4.2 The adapted BCG matrix

four or five in each area of the matrix. The items could come in categories such as *products* (things the school teaches, such as physical education), *processes* (key operating relationships such as the team work of the staff, working relationship with the governing body or communication with the community), *people* (individual qualities of members of staff), physical or financial *assets*.

A *star* is a highly successful or outstanding element of the school. For example, there may be an outstanding tradition in music in a secondary school or an exceptional teacher in the reception class in the primary school. A useful way of defining this is to consider what would be the two most outstanding things that you would want to show or explain to a visitor to the school.

An item is considered to be a *problem child* (or question mark) if it has the potential for success but, for some reason, that success has not yet materialised. The school is then faced with the choice of investing more time and resources in the hope of making it successful or of pulling out of the activity. An example of this is where a school has invested time and resources in establishing an extensive programme of after-school activities but the take-up has been limited. The school is faced with the difficult decision of withdrawing that resource and allocating it elsewhere or continuing with the investment (nurturing the child) in the hope that the take-up will be greater in the future.

A *cash cow* is an aspect of the school that is always reliable. This could be the Key Stage 1 literacy strategy which gets all children reading every year or it could be the reliable teacher who always does a good job even if she/he is not outstanding, someone about whom the senior leadership team do not have to worry. Cash cows are important as they do not require much resourcing and allow resources to be diverted to other aspects of the school's work. The danger is that, without any attention, these aspects may fall into decline.

Dogs are the unfortunate aspects of the school that are very unsuccessful or unpopular and present a major weakness in the school's operation. These are the areas that cause the school leadership the most problems; they demand action but quick solutions are not always possible. One example would be a minority language which is taught badly and/or has a poor take-up. Another might be the sports facilities of an inner-city school.

The use of the BCG matrix should involve two distinct but linked stages. First, using the best information available, the school's products, processes, people and assets are positioned on the matrix. This needs to be a focused activity. There is a danger of this turning into a 'therapy session' with endless lists in each category. Although the process may start off with a 'brain storming' session to generate many ideas or perspectives, it is important to agree at the start of the process to focus only on major and strategic issues and limit the number in each of the categories to four or five items.

Once this has taken place, the second strategic stage can begin. This is based on the following question: 'Assuming that the process is to be repeated in five years' time, what strategic capability-building exercises need to be carried out so that the positive elements (stars and cash cows) can be maintained into that future and the negative elements (problem children and dogs) can be either remedied or reduced?' This is shown in Figure 4.3.

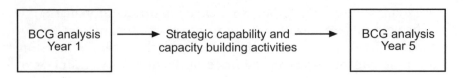

Figure 4.3 Using the BCG analysis to build strategic capability and capacity

The common action is to focus on the problem children or dogs, i.e. in five years' time we have solved the major problems and ensured that the things that aren't quite working are back on track. While this is obviously true, it is just as important to build a strategic perspective on what will sustain the reliable parts of the school (the cash cows) and the highly successful areas (the stars) so that they do not burn out. For example, one of the headteachers that we work with has formed a link with a US school in Philadelphia. He organises a teacher swap in the autumn half term so that he pays the airfare for one of his staff to visit and stay with a colleague in the US. There is no supply cover (as it is half term) and the teacher agrees to undertake reciprocal hosting of his/her American colleague in the spring. (Ironically, the cost of a return ticket to the East Coast of the USA in late October is about £300 less than the cost of a one-day course in London with supply cover.) The whole purpose is to make sure that the reliable members of staff who always do a good job do not get overlooked and can access world-class opportunities like this. So over a five-year period this is one of his staff development strategies to ensure that his cash cows don't turn into dogs!

A school using this BCG approach would use the strategic data which it has obtained in order to locate its products and processes on the matrix. Although, for convenience, we have placed items in discrete quadrants, in practice a product may be located across two or more quadrants. For example, technology may exhibit elements of star quality in that it provides leading-edge developments and has some very exciting work being achieved by the pupils. At the same time it could exhibit some elements of the 'problem child' as there may be serious problems in resourcing the replacement equipment and some staff may still be reluctant to engage fully in the use of technology in their teaching. In our case examples for primary and secondary schools (below), we have identified several school 'products' and located them on the matrix.

Case example: Primary school BCG

In this example, we have examined some of the school's provision. There are many aspects of its 'products' and 'processes' which could be considered and it would be possible to apply the analysis to 'people'.

STAR	PROBLEM CHILD
Information technology	Special needs provision
CASH COW	**DOG**
Basic literacy at Key Stage 1	Peripatetic music

Figure 4.4 Primary school BCG matrix

STAR

The star, as far as the school is concerned, is its information technology provision. It has invested heavily in turning its library area into a learning resource centre with a significant number of multi-media machines linked to the Internet. It has also organised a lease deal with a computer supplier for parents to buy a lap-top computer for their children over a three-year period. It is seen by parents as the leading school in the growing area of technology and, as a result, is significantly oversubscribed. The challenge is how to maintain the momentum and enthusiasm in this area and access sufficient resources to provide the high-level equipment and staff development necessary over the next five years.

PROBLEM CHILD

The problem child for this school is special needs. It does an excellent job with special needs children and has an enviable record in the area for its work. However, it does not believe the funding regime for special needs gives it adequate resources and it has to divert resources from other areas of the school. Continued success in this area over the next five years will exacerbate the resource problem. The school needs to engage in major change in strategic directions to determine the priority it gives this area and whether the resource dimension is solvable without major retrenchment of provision over the next five years.

CASH COW

The school's cash cow is basic literacy at Key Stage 1. The school has excellent learning schemes and achieves very good results in this area at Key Stage 1. As a result it retains a good impression with parents and secures an excellent intake for the school. The challenge is not to take the success and reliability in this area for granted but to reinforce continually its importance and not only sustain current efforts but to engage in major staff development into the nature of learning so that this area continues to be a corner-stone of the school's achievement in five years' time.

DOG

The dog product in this school is peripatetic music. The whole concept of extracting pupils for music tuition is disliked by children but the tutors are not available at any other time. Parents are increasingly dissatisfied with the quality of provision and the lack of stability of staffing so they are seeking alternative provision in the community. The school will need to decide whether this area needs to be completely reorganised to improve it radically.

Case example: Secondary school BCG

The analysis that follows relates to some of the school's provision. Many other aspects of its 'products', 'processes' and 'people' could be analysed and placed on the matrix.

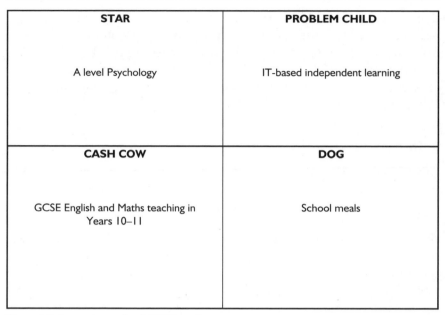

STAR	PROBLEM CHILD
A level Psychology	IT-based independent learning
CASH COW	**DOG**
GCSE English and Maths teaching in Years 10–11	School meals

Figure 4.5 Secondary school BCG matrix

STAR

The school has experienced a sustained and significant increase in pupils in the 6th form studying psychology. This could be considered to be a star product as there seems to be a growing market for this subject for a wide variety of careers and within the range of A/S levels offered it is taking an increasing share of option preferences. There are significant indications that more pupils are staying on because this option is available in the school. The key challenge over the next five years is to sustain this success and make sure that if a key teacher left there would be succession planning in place for a replacement.

PROBLEM CHILD

The school's problem child is its move to develop a greater focus on independent learning for pupils using various forms of information technology. At the moment it is a growing area with more and more quality software and other applications becoming available. The school, however, has to invest heavily in this development when it is short of resources. Also, the reluctance of teachers and parents to see this as an alternative to traditional teaching has meant that it takes a very low share of total learning and teaching time. Either the move to develop this area will lead to a significant expansion of both the range and quality of learning opportunities or it will become an expensive bolt-on facility to the traditional learning curriculum. The challenges for the school are how to change the professional culture and how to seek extra resourcing to move the situation on and stop this aspect becoming a 'dog' in the medium term.

CASH COW

The cash cows can be considered to be GCSE teaching in English and maths. The school is increasingly being judged on its literacy and numeracy outcomes at 16. Quality provision in these two subjects will ensure continued parental choice of the school and, hence, funding through the pupil unit component of the school budget. The danger here is that the leadership of the school focuses on the problems and ignores or takes for granted the reliable areas. There needs to be a conscious plan of activities to support and develop these areas over the next five years.

DOG

Like many organisations, the school has a few products which might be classified as 'dogs'. Here it is the school meals service. The school is situated near the middle of the town centre and pupils can choose from many alternative food sources at lunchtime. The present meals service is seen as expensive and the choices offered do not meet pupil expectations. The school needs to examine radical solutions such as changing contractors or only providing meals for 'free school meal entitlements' and abandoning the traditional meal service. The aim would be that over the next few years this ceases to be a problem.

The use of the BCG matrix

In both the primary and secondary examples, the strategic purpose of the activity is threefold. First, it provides a means of integrating the data gathered in the strategic analysis in order to determine the current position of key elements of the school's activities. Second, it focuses attention on action that needs to be undertaken to maintain star positioning, to ensure that problem children move to the left and not down to the dog category, to reinforce the core cash cow activities and, finally, to either damage limit or eliminate items in the dog category.

Third, the matrix can be used as a means of articulating what the school believes its products will be in five years' time and which categories they will be in. Most significantly, it should identify the problem children that require investment and development in the near future. There is a danger that, within a culture of short-term target-setting, instant solutions or 'quick fixes' are sought to difficult problems. In complex organisations like schools, problems are often multi-dimensional. Obvious solutions are not always easily found and it is necessary to build understanding first and courses of action second. The key idea with this strategic approach is to build the capacity and capability over a period of time (up to five years) as a means of developing sustainable solutions.

Exercise: Developing a BCG analysis

> 1. Identify the products, processes or people in your school which have emerged from the data gathering process (it is best to focus on a limited number such as two to four in each category) and place them on the BCG matrix.
> 2. Envisage how you would want the matrix to look in five years' time.
> 3. Discuss the strategic capability and capacity changes necessary to achieve the desired position in five years' time.

2. Comparative stakeholder analysis

As part of the strategic analysis, a school would collect data from four groups, the senior leadership, classroom teachers, the parents and governors, asking them to rate the school on a 1–10 scale against each of the criteria, as shown in the first column of Table 4.5. Each stakeholder group would not average the score but should agree on a score that is acceptable to all group members so that part of the activity is developing the art of strategic conversation. This is not a complete list of possible criteria; schools can change the list according to their own strategic agendas. The outcomes of such an analysis in a case study school are shown in Table 4.5.

The school should obviously focus on where there are low scores but the major significance may be where there is a different perception

Table 4.5 Comparative stakeholder analysis results

	Senior Leadership Team	Teachers	Parents	Governors
Educational results	7	7	4	5
Competition – other schools	6	5	8	5
Educational value added	7	8	6	5
Parental attitude to the school	8	7	6	7
Leadership and management skills	7	7	4	4
Quality of learning and teaching	4	7	5	4
Reputation	7	6	7	6
Location	4	3	8	5

by the different groups. Examples of the differences would be the perception of the results between the senior leadership team and teachers, for example regarding the quality of teaching and learning. Another significant difference is between the senior leadership team/ teachers and the parents/governors on the quality of leadership and management skills or the location of the school. There are several issues here. First, is the information about difference in opinion reflecting a fundamental weakness in the particular area or a difference in perception? This is very important. Is the strategic intention that the problem will be remedied or has the problem already been solved but the new situation needs better communication so that key groups are aware of it? Second, strategic analysis does not necessarily provide the answers but it provides strategic insights which still need intuition and judgement so that they can be interpreted before decisions can be made. Third, the discussion around the outcomes of the analysis, the strategic conversation, may be as important in developing a solution as the facts themselves.

It can be seen that this tool not only provides a means of bringing together the data and highlighting areas for attention in terms of high and low scores but it shows the different perceptions of the various stakeholder groups.

Exercise

> Using Table 4.5, as a member of the senior leadership team, rate your school against the criteria using the scoring of 1–10, then try to do the same using information from another participant's viewpoint.

3. SWOT analysis

Many schools or subject areas have used a SWOT analysis which considers strengths, weaknesses, opportunities and threats. Usually, the strengths and weaknesses are related to internal factors and the opportunities and threats relate to the external environment. In addition to its usual use to focus on a particular product or aspect of provision, a SWOT format can be used to compile a macro-picture from all the evidence gained through strategic analysis. This does not simply involve filling in the details from the data, but requires that senior leaders in the school consider the validity of the data gathered so that they provide valuable information. It is thus a more rational approach than the subjective use of the tool simply to gather stakeholders' perceptions.

The SWOT approach is quick and easy to carry out and does not require any special skill or equipment in order to carry it out or to analyse it. The tool can be made more sophisticated by introducing subcategories against which to place the information. This overcomes the criticism that, because of their diversity, the results cannot easily be summarised or aggregated. The information is not weighted so care must be taken in interpretation otherwise minor and major issues may be given equal prominence. Unlike some other tools, this process does not suggest any strategies other than the possibility of turning weaknesses into strengths and threats into opportunities.

In Table 4.6, we have used some of the subcategories which we suggest earlier in this chapter as aspects of the school's provision which should be covered by the data-gathering process.

Table 4.6 Initial criteria for a SWOT analysis

Internal factors	External factors
• Curriculum	• Political, legal and economic factors
• Learning and teaching	• Central/local educational changes
• Assessment and results	• Demographic and socio-cultural trends
• Extra-curricular activities	• Employment trends
• Discipline and appearance	• Technology
• Financial resources	• Customers
• Premises	• Other providers
• Staffing, staff skills and abilities	
• Governors	
• Ethos/culture	

At Brentwich School, the data-gathering exercise has been summarised as shown in Table 4.7.

Table 4.7 SWOT analysis for Brentwich School

	Strengths	**Weaknesses**
Curriculum	Literacy and language	Creative arts
Learning and teaching	Traditional approaches	Differentiation Extension materials for the more able
Assessment and results	Good use of baseline entry data. Steadily rising results in English	Targeting of individual performance. Maths results level over last 3 years
Extra-curricular activities	Sport	Few music or drama activities
Discipline and appearance	Clear behaviour policy	Inconsistent application of uniform policy
Financial resources	Balanced budget over last 2 years PTA income stable	Lack of partnership with wider business community to attract other funds
Premises	Welcoming entrance and reception area	Toilets need refurbishing
Staffing, staff skills and abilities	Considerable investment in staff development in the last five years	All school policies not applied consistently
Governors	Regularly attend meetings and school functions	Staff unhappy about their presence in lessons
Ethos/culture	Happy, willing pupils	Lack of shared vision and values, especially amongst staff

continued ...

Table 4.7 continued

	Opportunities	**Threats**
Political, legal and economic factors	Targeted funding increasing resources	Fewer quality teachers entering or remaining in the profession
Central/local educational changes	Further alterations to curriculum	Possibility of a new school on the other boundary of the estate. Increased focus on achievement of numeracy targets
Demographic and socio-cultural trends	New estate and new industrial complex should increase the local population	Cost of houses may mitigate against the families who might use this school
Employment trends	New developments in the area	Workers may commute because of the cost of housing
Technology	To harness technology to raise standards of numeracy	Cost and lack of staff skills
Customers	Community networks available to improve communication	Pressure to provide a wider range of art, music and drama facilities
Other providers	Dissemination of literacy skills to other providers within the region	Community perceptions and hopes of a new school

Exercise

Use the SWOT format as shown above and insert your own school's data.

Feasibility assessment

One of the key dilemmas in strategy is matching the desirability of a particular strategic change with the possibility of being able to implement that change in a particular time period, i.e is it feasible? In strategy, timing can be critical and the wisdom and intuition of the leader play a considerable role in judging not only what to do but when is the most appropriate time to do it. We have developed a model which can be used as a strategic analysis tool (see Davies and Ellison 1997b). We use it to interpret data into what could be considered a feasibility/desirability dimension which can be seen to operate as a matrix where the school's ability to provide (feasibility) is set against the perceived value to the client (desirability) as shown in Figure 4.6.

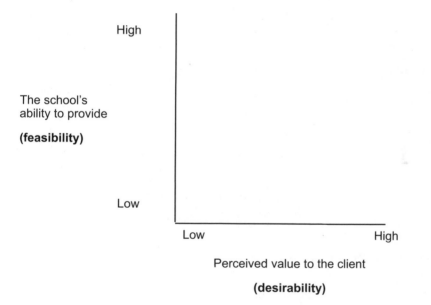

Figure 4.6 Feasibility and desirability matrix (adapted from Davies and Ellison 1997b: 217)

*Case example: A feasibility/desirability analysis of
Lincoln School's provision*

In Lincoln School the ability to provide sufficient high-quality information technology facilities is moderate (because of budget constraints)
while parental expectations in this area are high. Similarly, while
parents may consider Saturday morning games as very desirable, the
ability of the school to persuade staff to work on Saturday mornings
is very limited. The school can offer after-school music provision (for
a fee) and parents greatly value this. This situation is summarised in Figure
4.7.

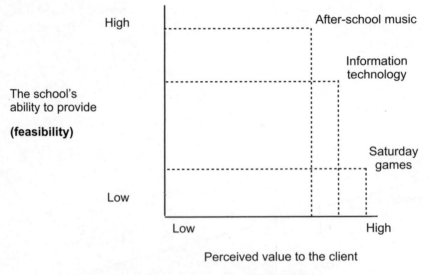

Figure 4.7 Feasibility and desirability matrix for Lincoln School

This type of analysis can be seen not only to relate the strategic
position between provider and receiver but also to define the feasibility
and suitability of various options.

Exercise

From the information which you have about your school:

1. Determine the features from the strategic analysis that you are considering implementing.
2. Decide on the school's capability (feasibility) to provide those features.
3. Decide on the desirability of those features in the eyes of the parents and pupils.
4. Position the features on the matrix.
5. Study the position of the features. Those that are high and to the right are the key ones in which the school can demonstrate effectiveness and the customer is keen to accept the feature. Those which are high and to the left may need special consideration in the planning and marketing process if the customer is to change his/her attitude to their value. For those features which appear elsewhere, the school needs to decide on the appropriate strategic alternatives.

High

The school's
ability to provide

(feasibility)

Low

Low   High

Perceived value to the client

(desirability)

Conclusion

This chapter has shown, initially, how to collect data, how to analyse data to build a strategic perspective so as to define strategic options and, finally, how to check whether those options are implementable. However, there is a danger that decisions will be made solely on the data gathered. We would suggest that the data and perceptions developed are used as the basis for a 'strategic conversation'. It is important to give time to reflect and debate on what has been found. Strategy has to be both a documented plan and also a way of thinking and developing a perspective that provides a context for daily decision-making. If colleagues in the school and the governing body are to develop a strategically focused school then providing opportunity to discuss and understand the strategic development needs of the school is as important as having a 'neat' plan. A good way of creating these strategic conversations is to separate out 'business matters' which deal with routine management and administration and 'policy matters' which deal with strategic developments. Indeed, several schools reflect this in their organisational structure. For example, Wise (2003) separates out team discussion through having open meetings which achieve this focus by adopting the following structure: (i) 'Operational Management Team' focusing on the next 0 to 12 months, (ii) 'School Development Plan Team' focusing on the next 6 to 24 months (iii) 'Strategic Research and Development Team' focusing on the next 2 to 5 years. These timescales are similar to our concept of 1 to 2 years for action planning and 3 to 5 years for strategic plans. While structure is important it is critical to provide the culture where strategic conversation can take place. Information is only useful if it is considered, reflected upon and discussed. Using this approach wise decisions are much more likely to emerge.

Chapter 5

Short-term action planning
Establishing a framework

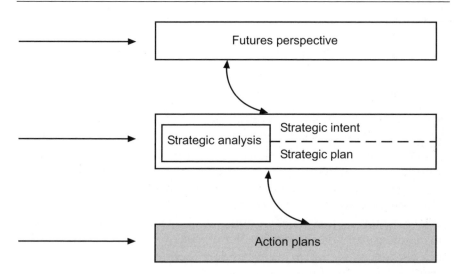

Introduction

The heads with whom we have been working have supported our view that the traditional school development plan should be replaced in two ways. The medium-term element is subsumed into the strategic plan (as outlined in Chapter Three). The shorter-term aspects of the plan should be in the form of clear, concise action plans which summarise outcomes and associated activities over a one- to two-year period. Action plans should focus on outputs, such as the raising of a particular aspect of pupil achievement or the introduction of a particular teaching or learning strategy. These plans would be created at a range of levels and areas of responsibility within the school, including the level of the individual teacher and pupil. While the focus on pupil progress and the raising of achievement has become the key organisational objective for schools, it is important that it is supported in the plan through the development of appropriate learning and teaching strategies and through effective leadership, management and resource deployment. This inclusion of all aspects of development would reflect the areas covered in the more strategic plans.

This chapter looks at this concept of short-term action plans which will support a demonstrable overall improvement in the quality of education and in pupil outcomes over a 12- to 24-month timescale. The chapter considers the functions of short-term action plans, the key pointers to success in creating and implementing them and our suggested framework. Schools will need to decide on appropriate terminology for this shorter-term planning; we have used action planning as this reflects the current emphasis in England. For the same reason, we have, on the whole, reserved the word 'target' for those specific outcomes that relate to pupils.

The functions of short-term action plans

While schools must aim for continuous improvement in the achievement of pupils, simply stating the desired outcomes or targets will not ensure that they are achieved. In order to provide a clear agenda for improvement, an action plan must also set out the processes which will support the achievement of the pupil targets. It is important to distinguish between pupil progress and achievement of particular outcomes, the factors which bring this about (e.g. effective learning and teaching) and the leadership and management activities to support both of these, based on an honest understanding of the school's current position. The school must begin by setting targets or goals for pupils and then specify activities and associated outcomes which will support the achievement of these pupil targets. The plans are used to ensure that the proposed activities are scheduled to be paced appropriately according to the school's capability, are resourced and, through their use as a checklist, that the planned activities do, in fact, take place in an effective manner. Effective short-term action plans have a number of purposes which are listed below and then developed in further detail.

- Specifying outcomes
- Involving stakeholders
- Prioritising tasks and focusing
- Allocating responsibilities
- Allocating resources
- Facilitating change

- Communicating
- Monitoring
- Annual reviewing and evaluating
- External accountability
- Recognition.

Specifying outcomes

The planning process enables the school to set challenging yet attainable and measurable outcomes for all aspects of its work in order to support continuous improvement in pupil learning and development. The setting of appropriate outcomes or targets for pupils is expanded upon later in this chapter, on pages 92–4.

A number of acronyms have been developed over the years in relation to outcomes and pupil targets. Guidance sometimes suggests the use of the term SMART in which the A represents 'achievable' and the R represents 'realistic'. We feel that these two really refer to the same thing so we use an adjusted version which should help to gain commitment and to encourage achievement. What is important in a school is that a similar list is agreed and used as a checklist during the action planning process. We feel that all outcomes and targets should be:

- Specific
- Measurable and monitored
- Achievable and agreed
- Relevant and resourced
- Timed
- Interesting
- Evaluated
- Success-orientated (and challenging).

Involving stakeholders

Many schools are now realising that the *process* of creating plans is vitally important for the achievement of the final '*product*' because it is through involvement in the development of plans that commitment is obtained for their realisation. Outcomes and pupil targets which have been agreed in advance are more likely to be achieved, so it is particularly important to involve pupils and staff in negotiating those that relate to them. The planning process can also involve parents and the wider community in partnership.

Prioritising tasks and focusing

At this operational stage, decisions are made about which activities, especially in relation to learning and teaching and the learning context, are the most important in order to improve the outcomes for pupils and which are more urgent than others. Realistic timescales with dates for achievement specified are needed according to resources available and an honest assessment of the school's capabilities and capacity (see Chapter Four). Timelines can be produced in a variety of ways in order to plot what needs doing and by when it must be completed. One of the most effective which we have seen for a large school was produced by Sedgefield Community College and involved using a database to sort the deadlines for activities by type, person or date. The costing of various alternative courses of action will allow the school to inform its decision-making process through 'value for money' information. Thus, the prioritising and focusing of effort is a key function of the action planning process.

Allocating responsibilities

Responsibility should be clearly allocated for the implementation, monitoring and evaluation of each of the actions in the plan so that outcomes are achieved in the relevant timescale. It is important to use expertise realistically, drawing on strengths and taking account of any shortcomings that there may be in capability. In order to spread the workload and provide development opportunities, responsibilities should be distributed amongst appropriate people. To avoid difficult situations or inaction, lines of accountability must be clear.

Allocating resources

The achievement of the planned outcomes requires the allocation of appropriate and adequate resources, both human and financial. The published plans will set out the allocation of financial resources and provide clear guidelines for spending and a framework for monitoring that expenditure. A weakness in many plans is that they fail to take account of the cost of human resources, so staff expertise and staff time for meetings, in service courses and so on should be costed (in money or in hours) and the cost of any external support should similarly be stated. It is important that the process of resource allocation should be seen as facilitating the educational process and explicit costing allows for cost-benefit and opportunity cost considerations to take place.

Facilitating change

A short-term action plan is part (along with the other, more strategic aspects of the overall plan) of the means of facilitating and driving through change in the school. It acts as a guide for those charged with the responsibility for carrying out the developments which are designed to allow the targets to be achieved. With a clear framework, staff can be supported to manage the changes by planning and prioritising their own work. The school can ensure that the staff are also supported in developing the appropriate skills and knowledge.

Communicating

Clear, concise action plans communicate what needs to be done across a variety of areas by providing a means of articulating and co-ordinating priorities and desired outcomes to all stakeholders. There is, thus, a coherent picture of the school's activities. This is very important if staff are to set their work in curricular areas, key stages, year teams, houses and so on in the overall context of the whole school priorities.

Monitoring

The plan can provide an effective instrument for monitoring progress both by those responsible for implementation and by those who have managerial oversight of the initiatives. A well thought out plan in which the outcomes are clearly specified, measurable and timed allows the school to assess where it is at various points in the year with respect to the outcomes and to ensure implementation. If they do not appear to be going to be achieved, remedial action can be undertaken before it is too late. In order that monitoring can be effective, the plan should state clearly how the progress of activities will be assessed and by whom. At the end of the primary school case study (Chapter Six) a proforma (linked to the plan) has been developed for reporting to governors.

Annual reviewing and evaluating

As a policy document approved by the governors, the whole-school action plan provides the basis of agreement and action by the stakeholders in the leadership and management of the school. By stating specific activities and outcomes, the plan provides a basis for annual review. The evaluation can ensure that the plan has been fully implemented or can investigate the reasons why certain aspects have been delayed or cancelled. As part of the planning process, the school must establish the structures and procedures by which a review will take place. As outcomes are achieved, new ones can be formulated for the next cycle of activity. Formal and planned evaluation can assist in the process of ensuring that the most effective means are chosen to reach the desired goals in the future.

External accountability

A short-term action plan provides part of the information for any external audit and evaluation of the school by the LEA or other external agency, such as OFSTED.

Recognition

A report on achievements or on progress can provide a major part of the information between the school and its stakeholders in signalling and proclaiming 'success'. The information can be disseminated at the governors' annual meeting, via newsletters or at parent/community activities.

Key pointers to success in short-term action planning

If it has been appropriately developed and if its content is relevant, then the short-term action plan is a concise, effective management and leadership tool which provides the mechanism for meeting short-term (annual) pupil-focused outcomes.

Our approach accommodates the criticism of planning made by Fullan who stated that 'the pursuit of planned change is a mug's game' because we exist in conditions of dynamic complexity so that 'most change is unplanned' (Fullan 1993: 138). By having the school's values and strategic intent as 'signposts', the action plan can be used to provide part of the path in the right direction in the short-term and can ensure that progress is made. Also, in terms of turbulence or change in the environment, then a 12- to 24-month time frame does give reasonable stability. While a longer-term framework of strategic planning is possible in some areas of the school's activities, the concept of strategic intent is more powerful in other areas. We believe that our model prevents an over-rigid approach by ensuring that, even while the operational plan is being created and implemented, there are people constantly scanning the environment in order to ensure that no valuable opportunities or shifts in direction are missed. We would also suggest that, despite the view of most staff, schools are relatively stable in terms of their *modus operandi*, staffing and budgets compared with most companies.

The OFSTED guidance on the creation of post-inspection plans (OFSTED 2001) is relevant here and given in Figure 5.1.

The most successful action plans are likely to concentrate on improving:

- the leadership provided by the headteacher and key staff, including governors, with particular emphasis on their strategies for raising standards;
- levels of attainment;
- management, including pastoral care of pupils/staff, communication, financial planning, control and administration;
- systems to monitor and evaluate the school's performance;
- the pupils' behaviour, attitudes and work habits;
- the planning and organisation of lessons;
- the challenge and pace of learning;
- the quality and range of opportunities for learning including the development of policies, schemes of work, curricular planning, and assessment, recording and reporting;
- resources to address the above.

Figure 5.1 OFSTED guidance on the creation of post-inspection plans (OFSTED 2001)

An effective action plan should involve everyone at all levels in the school so it should comprise a range of specific activities and outcomes for:

- the whole school, taking account of national, local and school priorities;
- subject areas and other sub-units;
- staff – in order to achieve the whole-school and area outcomes;
- pupils – who set targets in order to ensure that achievement is raised to an appropriate level.

We explain our approaches to planning at these various levels later in this chapter and they can be seen in the case examples in Chapters Six to Eight.

Plans should be based on evidence gathered during the strategic analysis (see Chapter Four). They should focus on a limited number of activities in order to make it more likely that they are achieved. A 12- to 24-month period is appropriate with regular reviews. Clear, concise and unambiguous plans are needed so that outcomes and success criteria are clear and disagreement can be avoided. The layout of the document should show clearly:

- details of the activities that contribute to achieving the strategic intent and the strategic plan;
- costings for each activity;
- clear responsibilities for implementation and for monitoring;
- clear success criteria for each target.

Plans should be live documents and should not lie unused on a shelf. They should be checked at frequent intervals and any necessary adjustments should be made. The mistake is to think of a plan as being written once and that the only change is one year later. Plans can and should be updated as circumstances change. As our colleague, Brian Caldwell, says, in changing times, a plan should not be regarded as an immutable document.

The importance of involvement in the process of deciding on outcomes and pupil targets cannot be underestimated. Pupils will over-achieve on targets they set for themselves so their involvement is critical to success, although schools and LEAs are under considerable pressure to ensure that their aggregated targets contribute to the achievement of national goals. A similar commitment can be gained by involving staff and other stakeholders in setting outcomes for activities which apply to them.

The framework

In order to fulfil the criteria discussed above, we have devised a short-term action planning approach which has activities and outcomes at four interlinked levels:

- whole school
- area
- individual staff
- individual pupils.

The links are shown in Figure 5.2 and we outline our thinking in each of these areas.

The whole-school action plan

The process of developing this plan will be led by the school's senior staff and should involve a dialogue with other stakeholders. Schools will decide on activities and outcomes for which they can take responsibility and which they feel can be achieved, while ensuring that they work towards achieving overall and longer-term targets set by the government.

There should be a limited number of whole-school activities to ensure focus and the primary ones should relate to improved learning outcomes. There is a variety of sources of information or evidence to be considered when deciding on whole-school activities.

1. An obvious starting point would be to review the progress made on the previous year's plan in order to ensure that earlier work and successes are built upon and extended.

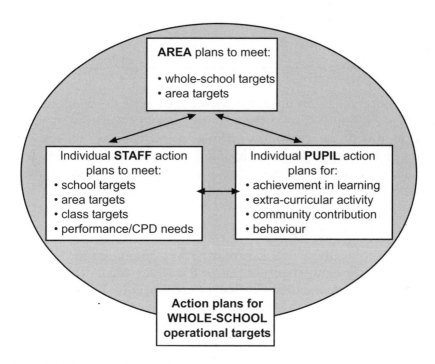

Figure 5.2 The types of action plan

2. Reference to the school's strategic intent framework and strategic plan may point to new areas to be tackled.
3. Recent changes to legislation or to parental expectations will also demand certain action. For example, plans will need to take account of national goals for attainment, national strategies for improvement and so on.
4. Factors relating to new pupils entering the school will need to be considered as they may have different prior attainment and future needs to existing pupils.

Taberrer (1997) points out that it is important to link the desired outcomes for pupils to the processes or activities listed in the plans so that approaches to learning and teaching and changes to leadership, resources and so on are not seen as a means to an end.

Table 5.1 Linking desired outcomes to the action plan

Improved learning outcomes	Relevant process in action plan
Add *x* to pupils' reading achievement	Evaluate literacy strategies
	Strengthen and guarantee the home reading support
	Provide additional classroom assistance

It is important to set up processes for reviewing the whole-school plan. Some schools allocate the responsibility to a senior member of staff, often with a governor also taking an interest. In other schools, there can be a task-force monitoring progress on each activity. It is very important that regular review takes place in order to confirm that progress is being made or to initiate remedial action.

The area action plans

Each area of the school should produce two planning sheets. One will demonstrate the team's contribution to the achievement of the whole-school action plan and the other will be area specific. Schools will, by their very nature, have different ways of defining 'area' because of their types of internal organisation or grouping. For example, a primary school will probably do much of its standards-related action planning based on achievement in National Curriculum subject areas for particular age ranges. Each year group or class will do further, more detailed planning. The school will need to decide which types of plans will be written in order to make the most effective use of teachers' time. Our example shows those for science. In a secondary school there will certainly be faculty and/or department plans but there will be a variety of other groupings depending on the way in which the school is organised. These may include cross-curricular aspects, houses, year groups, key stages and so on.

Each area will review its plans and achievements for the previous year and will consider its own development needs and those of the whole school. It will then plan activities and outcomes in order to make its contribution to the achievement of the whole-school plan and its own needs. The area will need to decide who is responsible for ensuring that each activity is implemented and will set up its own system of monitoring to ensure that progress is being made throughout the year. When the area plans are complete, they will then link to a key part of each member of staff's individual plan.

The individual staff plans

Each member of staff should demonstrate his/her contribution to the success of both whole-school and area plans. The performance management process requires that the teacher demonstrates his/her contribution to the achievement of pupil targets so professional development targets will be set for each member of staff in order to support them in making this contribution and to assist them in developing their careers. Similarly, each member of staff will contribute to the personal development of a group of pupils through providing support and monitoring progress. Thus, an individual member of staff is responsible for:

- contributing to the achievement of the whole-school plan
- making a major contribution to the area activities and outcomes
- implementing plans at the classroom level and monitoring pupil targets
- taking responsibility for his/her own continuing professional development (CPD).

The proforma on page 101 is intended to stimulate a strategic dialogue about the member of staff's contribution, targets and development needs.

Pupil targets

While governors have a statutory responsibility with regard to setting targets for pupil attainment in SATs, we are focusing here on the process of working with individual pupils.

Much work has been done in schools on the creation of Individual Education Plans for statemented pupils. In addition, many schools across the age range have put considerable effort into Records of Achievement so that pupils are encouraged to record their interests and achievements and to propose areas for action. Most secondary schools have worked with examination pupils (especially those at the C/D grade boundary for GCSE!) in order to help them to work towards particular grade profiles and primary schools have implemented a range of strategies to raise success at Key Stage 2. What is needed is a bringing together of these initiatives and a partnership with parents so that each pupil is involved in setting some targets which provide a challenge. Although we show examples on pages 102 and 103, there will be considerable differences for pupils across the age range and it may be valuable to involve pupils in the design of an appropriate proforma. Support and regular monitoring should ensure that each child is challenged to reach his/her full potential, both academically and in terms of involvement in a broad curricular and extra-curricular diet of activity.

Although the use of appropriate language would be important, the plan could include targets for:

- achievement in learning
- extra-curricular activity
- community contribution
- behaviour.

In a secondary school, each pupil should have a mentor who will offer support and monitor progress. This may be the class or form teacher or another appropriate person. In a primary school, the class teacher will have regular contact with the pupil and can offer support as needed.

Targets for achievement

Taberrer (1997) describes three types of targets which could be developed and which would provide specific and measurable targets:

1. *Elite targets*, for example, targets relating to a greater number of pupils achieving a particularly desirable target such as more with 5 A*–C grades at GCSE or more achieving at Level 3 at the end of Key Stage 1.
2. *Average targets* such as a greater percentage of the year group achieving Level 4 at the end of Key Stage 2. The DfES system is based on the setting by each school of average targets for each key stage.
3. *Reliability targets* such as a reduction in the number of pupils 'failing', for example that there should be no non-readers at age 7 or no children with no A*–C grades at GCSE.

Schools will need to decide whether to set targets of different types. If only average targets are used, this may lead to a lack of attention to the pupils at the upper and lower ends of the ability range. A mix of types will ensure that the challenge affects all pupils.

Challenging targets

In order to plan achievable but challenging targets, it will be necessary to benchmark against other schools. This process will need to take account of the differences and similarities between schools. For example, a particular school with a similar intake could be chosen for detailed examination and the comparative data provided on a range of schools could be used in a more general sense. This could, however, provide a minimalist rather than a challenging approach. Those schools who really wish to promote challenge and raise achievement will keep up-to-date about what is being achieved by other schools in the world, rather than just to benchmark against national or local norms. They will also consider what can be achieved using non-traditional approaches to learning. Targets which are set within the comfort zone (Figure 5.3) are not especially challenging in themselves but may be appropriate if the pupils are tackling more challenging targets in other subjects. The SMART zone represents the setting of targets which are challenging and where the school is trying to make a real difference in attainment. In order to ensure that targets are achievable, it is better to be realistic about capability and not to set too many targets in this zone. The 'unlikely' zone speaks for itself. Whilst 'wild' targets *can* be achieved under certain circumstances, failure can be very demoralising for pupils and staff.

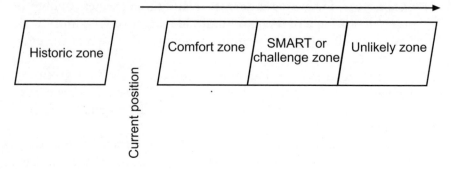

Figure 5.3 Progress towards targets (based on DFEE 1977: 14)

The pupil targets will be linked to the whole-school targets in a number of ways:

- Whole school targets will be an aggregation of the individual targets;
- Departments/areas will have to plan to deliver on the targets and will be accountable for their achievement;
- Staff will take part in professional development activities in support of the targets;
- Management activities will be linked to pupil need, e.g. in ensuring resources for the provision of appropriate technology, well maintained premises, sporting facilities, staffing structures.

While some general considerations relating to targets and target-setting are outlined here, more detail can be found in government publications such as *Setting Targets to Raise Standards* (DFEE, 1996) and *From Targets to Action* (DFEE, 1997).

Completed examples of short-term action plans are reproduced in Tables 5.2–5.7 and Figures 5.4–5.6 and blank proforma are included in the Appendix.

Case examples of a primary school and a secondary school are included as Chapters Six and Seven. Their completed planning documents show how two schools have adapted our framework to suit their own needs.

Table 5.2 Whole-school action plan 2003/2004: Primary school example

Target	Responsibility	Cost	Desired outcome	Completed by	Reviewed by
1. Devise and implement revised scheme of work for science	Science subject leader	£	Well planned science lessons, appropriately resourced	Sept 2003	Headteacher
2. 80% of pupils in Year 5 to have a reading age at least as high as their chronological age	Literacy co-ordinator	£ £	Active support of parents and use of literacy hour to ensure 80% reach the target in standardised tests. Begin action research project	July 2004 Jan 2004	Leadership Team
3. 80% of pupils in Year 2 to reach Level 2 in maths; 20% to reach Level 3	Maths co-ordinator	£	More direct teaching, use of IT and extension activities to ensure SAT results as per target.	June 2004	Leadership Team
4. Implement new system of recording pupil progress	Assessment co-ordinator	£	Data readily available when required from class teachers	Jan 2004	Headteacher
5. Further develop school library area	Literacy co-ordinator	£	Decorated, furniture repaired, computer area with 6 sockets	April 2004	Deputy Head
6. Displays of work to celebrate pupil achievement and stimulate learning	Art subject leader	£	Opportunity for all pupils to have work displayed in a stimulating environment	Dec 2003	Deputy Head

Table 5.3 Primary: Science action plan Part I – to meet whole-school action plan 2003/2004

Whole-school target	Actions/tasks/strategies	Respons-ibility	Who involved?	Cost	Inset	Desired outcome (how know achieved?)	Completed by	Monitored by?
2. Literacy – Y5	Non-fiction science texts used in literacy hour. Creation of science-focused word bank	Science subject leader	Y5 Class teacher Literacy co-ordinator	£	One day 'using literacy hour creatively'	Year 5 pupils to use science vocabulary appropriately	Dec 2003	Literacy co-ordinator
3. Numeracy – Y2	To ensure pupils have the opportunity to present data appropriately; applying that learnt in mathematics	Science subject leader	Maths co-ordinator Y2 Class teacher	£		Pupils able to apply maths teaching to record scientific investigations	April 2004	Maths co-ordinator
4. Recording system	Identify key learning objectives for year group science plans. New assessment recording format introduced for science	Science subject leader	Assessment co-ordinator Class teachers	£	Staff training day	Records used to record achievements and identify areas of difficulty against key learning objectives	Dec 2003	Assessment co-ordinator
5. School Library	Review library stock for science. Target spending for next cycle of science topics. Monitor and evaluate use and effectiveness	Science subject leader	Class teachers	£		Appropriate books available for all science-focused curriculum elements	Feb 2004	Literacy co-ordinator
6. Display	Science work to be displayed to value children's efforts and achievements. New work supported with interactive display	Science subject leader	Class teachers	£	Discuss at staff meeting	Children feel their learning in science is celebrated. Children use interactive displays in classrooms for information, new challenge and problems	Dec 2003	Art subject leader

Table 5.4 Primary: Science action plan Part 2 – to develop subject area 2003/2004

Subject area target	Actions/tasks/strategies	Respons-ibility	Who involved?	Cost	Inset	Desired outcome (how know achieved?)	Completed by	Monitored by
1.	Write new scheme of work to take account of new curriculum	Science subject leader	Class teachers	£	Staff meetings	Scheme used for class planning	Dec 2003	Headteacher
2.	Monitor planning to ensure continuity and progression	Science subject leader	Class teachers	£	Staff meeting	Science year plans take account of previous learning and demonstrate progression	July 2004	Leadership team
3.	Monitor and evaluate use and effectiveness of science resources	Science subject leader	Key stage co-ordinators	£		Evidence of more science equipment used in classrooms and centralised storage effective	April 2004	Deputy Head
4.	Investigate staff and pupils' attitudes to science	Deputy Head	Children and Class teachers	£		Children think of themselves as scientists. Staff positive about own knowledge and teaching	May 2004	Leadership team
5	Monitor and evaluate teaching and learning against agreed criteria	Headteacher	Class teachers	£	INSET day	Science taught effectively, pace and challenge in lessons, tasks matched to ability	July 2004	Governors
6.	Update school 'levelness portfolio'	Assessment co-ordinator	Governors Class teachers	£		Common understanding of standards	May 2004	Headteacher
7.	Prepare Governors for school visit to monitor and evaluate science practice	Subject leader	Governors Class teachers	£	After-school workshop for staff and Governors	Governors informed about approach, policy and practice	Sept 2004	Headteacher

Table 5.5 Secondary school example – Whole-school action plan 2003/2004

	Target	Responsibility	Cost	Desired outcome	Completed by	Reviewed by
1.	Improve levels of literacy	Kathryn Smith (Head of English)		70% of pupils in Year 9 to reach Level 5 in English	May 2004	HOD English/ Headteacher
2.	Improve levels of numeracy	Barry Price (Head of Maths)		71% of pupils in Year 9 to reach Level 5 in Maths	May 2004	HOD Maths/ Headteacher
3.	Improve higher grade results at GCSE	Gill Davies (Head of KS4)		58% pupils to achieve 5 A*–C at GCSE	June 2004	KS4 Co-ordinator/ Deputy Head 1
4.	Improve standards of teaching	Simon Jones (i/c staff development)		Variety of styles used including IT, 90% lessons rated good or above	July 2004	Deputy Head 2
5.	Improve attendance in KS4	Lorna Crowther (HOY10)		Electronic registration operating effectively; 95% attendance in Y10	Nov 2003; July 2004	KS4 Co-ordinator
6.						
7.						
8.						
9.						

Table 5.6 Secondary: Science action plan Part 1 – to meet whole-school action plan 2003/2004

Whole-school target	Actions/tasks/strategies	Respons-ibility	Who involved?	Cost	Inset	Desired outcome (how know achieved?)	Completed by	Monitored by
1. Literacy – Y9	Creation of science dictionaries	Bill Desmond (i/c KS3 Science)	all staff		2 hour meeting on training day	Pupils understand meaning of words and can spell them – each has growing dictionary	July 2004	HOD
2. Numeracy – Y9	Regular use of calculations	Bill Desmond	all staff	nil	Normal planning time	Calculations used at least once a month	in operation by Nov 2003	HOD
3. GCSE results	Use existing data to set targets and mentor	Jane Hunter (i/c KS4 Science)	all staff	staffing for review time	1 day plus 2 hours for faculty	4 review points in Y11	Oct 2003	HOD
4. Teaching quality	Peer review – varied styles, interest, differentiation and pace (further targets in this area next year)	Jean Percy (HOD)	all staff	staff time – 12 times 1 day,	2 hours on training day for peer review; pace and learning styles covered last year	All staff have observed 2 others and discussed styles	May 2004	HOD/DH 2
5. Attendance KS4	Monitor attendance and follow-up absence; Ensure that lessons are interesting	Jane Hunter	all staff	normal procedure		Whole-school systems implemented and utilised; 90% lessons rated good or above	Jan 2004	HOD/KS4 Co-ordinator

Table 5.7 Secondary: Science action plan Part 2 – to develop subject area 2003/2004

Area-specific target	Actions/tasks/strategies	Respons-ibility	Who involved?	Cost	Inset	Desired outcome (how know achieved?)	Completed by	Monitored by
1. Sixth Form	Review progress with new courses – improve pupil target-setting	Jane Hunter	JH, LC, SJ	3 × 1 hour meetings	–	Improved student exam grades	April 2004	Jean Percy
2. KS3	Review and extend opportunities for more practical work, especially in physical science	Bill Desmond	SN, WG, AH	6 × 1 hour meetings	–	20% increase in experimental work in Years 8 and 9 compared with 2002/2003	Feb 2004	Jean Percy
3. Incorporation of ICT into lessons	Staff development, shadowing; equipment in all labs	Stuart Nuttall	all staff	£	time for shadowing, 5 × 1 hour workshops in directed time	each class using IT as a tool at least 6 times a year e.g. for control, measurement, calculation, display	July 2004	Jane Hunter
4. New gas and water taps	New fittings in S1–S4	Matthew Green	–	£	–	fitting completed without disrupting lessons	March 2004	Jean Percy
5. Improve staff Health and Safety Awareness	1 day on H & S regulations; 1 day first aid course	Matthew Green (technician)	all teaching and technician staff	£	use training days	greater awareness of issues; 20% staff moving on to accredited courses, e.g. First Aid at Work	Feb 2004	Jean Percy

PERFORMANCE REVIEW/INDIVIDUAL STAFF TARGETS

NAME	PERIOD
Subject/Year/KS Group	Reporting to

OVERVIEW/CONTEXT/ QUESTIONS	INDIVIDUAL SPECIFIC TARGETS	BY WHEN	REV BY
Phase One			
1. What contribution did you make to whole-school plans last year?	1.		
2. What contribution did you make to your area of responsibility (subject, year group, key stage, etc.)?	2.		
Phase Two	3.		
1. What contribution will you make to whole-school plans next year?	4.		
2. What contribution will you make to your area of responsibility (subject, year group, key stage, etc.)?	5.		
Phase Three	6.		
What support do you need to achieve your targets for next year?			

Targets should relate to   whole school
     area
     pupil
     own CPD

Figure 5.4 Individual staff plan

PUPIL PERSONAL ACTION PLAN

NAME Peter Duncan	ACTION PLAN FOR PERIOD
CLASS Mrs Morrison	............Autumn 2003............

What I would like to become better at	How do you think you could do this?	Who needs to help you?	What do you need to help you to do this?	When will you do it by?	Teacher comment
In School					
Spelling	Read more books	Mum Mrs Morrison	Reminders Quiet time	Christmas	We will keep a chart
8 times table	Say it each day	Mum Mrs Morrison	Tests	November	I will test you
Out of school					
Score more goals	Practise after school	Dad My mates	Practice time	November	
	Go on holiday scheme		Place on scheme		See Mr ·Taylor

Figure 5.5 Pupil action plans – primary

PUPIL PERSONAL ACTION PLAN

NAME *Rebecca Kemp*	**ACTION PLAN FOR PERIOD** *......Sept. 2003 to July 2004......*
CLASS *9LP*	**CLASS TEACHER/PERSONAL TUTOR** *Mrs Pickthall*

TARGET	ACTION PLANNED	BY WHEN?	COMMENT
Achievement in learning			
Improve homework marks – nothing below C/B	Stay after school 2 days a week Write at desk Keep homework diary up-to-date	October 31st	A good plan
Extra-curricular activity			
Learn lifesaving Join drama group	Join classes on Saturdays Join Tuesday lunchtime at school	October 1st joined both	See Mrs Hibbert
Community contribution			
Sponsored event for charity	Organise for the class with 2 friends	February	We can plan this in PSHE
Behaviour/Personal Skills			
Improve punctuality in mornings	Set alarm No late marks	December 1st	Excellent idea

Figure 5.6 Pupil action plans – secondary

Chapter 6

Primary school case study

Barbara Davies

Introduction

While the Appendix shows planning proforma for our model, we would encourage schools to use these as a basis to develop their own frameworks and not to follow our design slavishly. Barbara J. Davies is one of the leading headteachers who has used our model as a way of thinking but who has adapted the documentation to create a new planning framework that meets the needs of Tuxford Primary and Nursery School. Using this framework between 2000 and 2002, the planning process at Tuxford was transformed and was the cornerstone of a successful OFSTED inspection.

To set up a coherent planning process for the school, Barbara led the development of a planning process which comprised six elements:

1. A contextual statement about the nature of planning at the school
2. A futures thinking statement based on a set of beliefs
3. A series of strategic intents
4. A three-year strategic plan based on five key areas for improvement
5. An operational plan (action plan) for a one-year period
6. A restructured headteacher's report format for governors, based on the planning framework

It is significant that the head notes, on the first page, that the process of planning is as important as the plan itself. This is reinforced by her view that the aims of the planning *process* are stated. The plan which we show in this chapter was created by the head and the staff working collaboratively with governors. We are grateful for Barbara's cooperation in producing this chapter and for the permission of the governors of Tuxford Primary and Nursery School to publish it.

This was the first year that the planning process was carried out in this way, so its timescales can be seen to fit the model as in Figure 6.1. The Head recognises that, following review of the process, there may be some changes to this perspective.

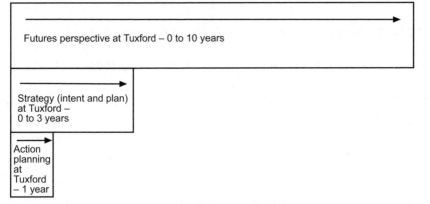

Figure 6.1   Tuxford Primary and Nursery School timescales

When considering the tables in the strategic and action plans, it should be noted that not all strategic improvement objectives are followed through into the first year's action plan and that some additional short-term objectives appear only in the action plan as they are issues which have arisen as priorities.

Table 6.1 Key to initials used in Tuxford Primary and Nursery School plan

SLT	School leadership team
HT	Headteacher
DHT	Deputy headteacher
SENCo	Special Educational Needs Co-ordinator
SL	Subject leader
KSC	Key stage co-ordinator
CC	Community co-ordinator
CT	Class teacher
Fin Of	Finance officer
SDC	Strategic Development Committee (of governors)
PP	Pupils and Personnel Committee (of governors)
SEN	Special Educational Needs
PD	Professional development
ASD	Autistic spectrum disorder
IEP	Individual education plan
LTP/MTP/STP	Long-, medium- and short-term planning
PM	Performance management
SIP	School improvement plan
NOF	New Opportunities Fund (provision of ICT training)
KI	Key Issue (from HMI report, June 1999)

Note Other initials refer to subjects, e.g. PE, PSHE.

Tuxford Primary and Nursery School
Planning for School Improvement

1. The Context of Planning at Tuxford Primary School

Review of Previous Practice (September 1999 – May 2000)

The existing one-year plan was based on key issues identified by OFSTED and HMI teams. This one-year plan was devised by the Headteacher with further actions decided by each individual teacher identified, on the plan, as being responsible for each key issue. Financial implications were recorded but the budget decisions, made by the budget manager, were based on historical practice.

Aims of the Current Planning Process

To recognise that the planning process has a key role in the translation of our aims and values into practice. It will give our school a clear direction and a sense of team purpose. The process is as important as the actual document.

To create a plan, underpinned by sound financial planning, which identifies priorities and targets for ensuring that pupils achieve high standards and make progress.

To establish the importance of development planning not just for the short-term, i.e. the school's one-year action plan, but also for the achievement of our medium-term and long-term goals.

To establish the process for creating a school improvement plan which involves governors, staff, parents and children. To establish this process as a sequence of activities: initial analysis, identification of needs, prioritisation of actions, monitoring of progress and evaluation of outcomes leading to a review and redefinition of the plan.

Our Definition of Planning

We see considerable confusion in the terms and concepts of planning, so for our purposes we see planning as encompassing:

1) **Annual Operational Plans** – traditionally labelled 'School Development Plans', these can spread over one or two years but then link into strategic plans.

2) **Strategy**, which consist of Strategic Intent, and Strategic Plans (see Boisot 1995; Davies and Ellison 1999; DfEE 2001; Hamel and Prahalad 1989). We define strategy as broad areas for action dealing with aggregated data on a medium-term time scale. We do not see that adding year after year of detailed plans makes those plans strategic. We see *strategic planning* as broad development areas where the targets are known and the actions necessary to achieve those targets are also understood. We see *strategic intents* as targeted changes where the capability has first to be built, through a series of understandings and activities, before detailed planning can commence. Both are underpinned by strategic thinking.

3) **Futures Thinking**. We consider this by taking the longer-term view where a futures dialogue or perspective is built up. A useful way of thinking about this is that a nursery child joining us in 2001 will not leave Year 6 until 2008 and we must develop a dialogue among the school community to define what experiences we need to provide for that child in the last year that the child is with us. Thus a 7–10 year framework is valuable for these purposes.

Planning Objectives May 2000 – August 2001

- To identify a futures view of the way that we see our school in 5–10 years' time, and identify what we are doing now which will have the biggest effect on what happens then.
- To identify and prioritise objectives for school improvement.
- To identify a strategy which includes a strategic plan and strategic intent.
- To involve staff and governors in the process.
- To convert the intentions into an operational action plan which gives an holistic overview.
- To create and implement a framework for monitoring and evaluating the improvements and the process.

How we Define the Terms in our Planning Document

Evaluation will take place after monitoring and will help us assess the quality of what we have done, whether the action has made a difference and what we need to do next.

Improvement Objective (IO) is the focus for what we want to achieve.

Key Action is the detailed activity which operationalises the improvement objective.

Monitoring is to ensure that actions have taken place as planned.

Success Criteria (SC) are how we detect our achievements. Some of these are quantifiable but some of what we value is not, thus 'detectable' encompasses achievements which are quantifiable and achievements which are value driven.

2. Futures Thinking

We will work in the future to enact a set of beliefs

We believe that our school will be a community where:

- all will be involved with working towards the same goals;
- all will improve on our previous bests;
- our core purpose is to enable effective learning in all we do;
- all will believe in the potential of each child.

We believe that each child's needs are at the centre of all we do so that:

- children will be willing, autonomous learners with positive attitudes to learning;
- each child will be an individual, be independent, thinking and responsible;
- children will feel involved and take an active role in the processes of the school.

We believe that our learning environment will:

- be stimulating, inviting, interactive, safe and a pleasant place to be;
- provide for all the resources appropriate for the job;
- allow parents, staff, governors, outside agencies and the wider community to work with us in partnership.

We believe that parents will:

- have more involvement;
- see the day as a learning day, not 'the school day', using ICT and library resources.

We believe that staff will:

- feel part of a happy, valued team, supported by each other;
- have opportunities for professional development and talk about their learning;
- have high expectations of themselves, each child and each other;
- have shared understandings of values and standards.

3. Strategic Intents

We will undertake a series of activities in each of the following intent areas to build our understanding of what is needed to achieve each intent and then, with that understanding, we will formulate a plan to sustain successful change.

A   Create a success culture: celebrate success

1. Two items at the end of the day, each class. Lesson objective build up every day.
2. STAR assembly book to include Nursery and displayed.
3. Impressions of our school book.
4. Newsletter – one per half term. Tuxfordian – contribution to each issue.
5. Displays/learning environment improvement.
6. Success messages used by all.
7. Staff meetings used to celebrate success.
8. Behaviour rewards – leaves on the hall tree.

B   Develop a shared understanding of high achievement and standards

1. Define what success is.
2. Benchmark standards – internal book of levels/external visits to other schools/internal visits to other year groups.
3. Feedback to parents – what are we achieving?
4. Recording and reporting progress of individual children.

C   Involving parents in the success culture, with a focus on learning

1. Contribution to newsletter/Tuxfordian.
2. Support and promote PFA.
3. Parent workshops N to Y6 for key areas.

D   Design and implement accurate performance indicators – use data to inform practice

1. Pupils setting own targets, 1 per term.
2. Achievements of school plan identified and focus for reporting system.
3. Use of data already collected to identify 'focus' groups.
4. Data to be used at school, class and individual level.

E   Develop a shared understanding of an effective team

1. Include Governors in INSET.
2. Involve all staff in behaviour focus.

3. Celebrate achievements of whole team – feedback session.
4. Involve all in 'motto' building. What are we committed to?
5. Mutually supportive/positive work environment.
6. Define what an effective team is.
7. Define high performance and expectations.
8. Create a shared view.
9. Maintain morale/focus on success.
10. Develop shared understanding of corporate responsibility.
11. Develop team approach to developments by establishing school/ leadership teams.
12. Opportunities for individuals to develop.

F   Create a positive and aesthetic learning environment

1. Initial impact/first impressions.
2. Display change timetable.
3. Standards defined.
4. Parents/children notice-board.
5. Develop rewards for personal bests.
6. All adults modelling behaviour – attitudes expected.
7. Written policy.
8. Staff meeting held in classrooms to share good practice.

G   Celebrate the school in the wider community

1. Establish communication group.
2. Ensure all communications focus the positive – written and verbal.
3. Whole team understands the way forward and what we want to achieve.

H   Focus on learning

1. Establish learning board in staff room.
2. To develop key skills through operational targets.
3. To develop children's work habits.
4. Recording and reporting process.

I   Involve children in processes/responsibility

1. Set up School Council with representative from each class.
2. Identify whole-school 'jobs' and responsibilities.

4. Strategic Plan 2000–2003

Improvement Area 1: Educational Standards	Who?	Phased action areas to achieve strategy; indicative costs					
		2000–2001		2001–2002		2002–2003	
IO1: To improve standards of pupil achievement in reading and writing. SC: Children achieving their individual targets to rise from 80% to 85% by 2003.	SL	• Set individual targets • Establish target groups • Improve presentation	3500	• Tests/Analysis of data • Resources • Parent workshops • Book of levels expectations • Planning • THRASS • Policy	4500	• Creative approach to curriculum links • Application of learning and teaching policy	4500
IO2: To improve standards of pupil achievement in mathematics. SC: Children achieving their individual targets to rise from 80% to 85% by 2003.	SL	• Set individual targets • Establish target groups • Improve presentation	400	• Tests/Analysis of data • Resources • Book of levels expectations • Tests • Planning	2000	• Parent workshops • ICT links • Policy • Application of learning and teaching policy	3000
IO3: To develop a positive approach to children's behaviour and behaviour management by all staff. SC: Consistency in children's behaviour and staff response to it.	HT	• Children responsible • Conflict management • Social competence • Midday staff involvement • Celebrate success, build self esteem • Rules and responsibilities • PSHE policy	600	• Focus on appreciation of others' needs, views and feelings • Targeting positive behaviour • Listening to children • Rewards and sanctions • Anti-bullying	600	• Kitchen staff involvement • Emotional competence	300

Improvement Area 2: Children	Who?	Phased action areas to achieve strategy; indicative costs					
		2000–2001		2001–2002		2002–2003	
IO1: To improve attendance. SC: Rate of attendance to rise to 95% by 2003.	HT	• Target groups • Letters to parents • Celebration of 100%	50	• Systems for contact • Children's views	50		
IO2: To develop an effective inclusion policy, so all children who experience difficulties in learning enjoy the same rights in our school. SC: Policy for inclusion actively seen in practice.	SENCo	• SEN Planning • SEN Process • SEN Policy • SEN Resources	1500	• SEN able children • Establish how well different groups do in school, i.e. gender, culture • Inclusion Policy • Child protection	1500	• Application of learning and teaching policy	1500

Phased action areas to achieve strategy; indicative costs

Improvement Area 3: Educational Standards	Who?	2000–2001		2001–2002		2002–2003	
IO1: To improve the quality of learning. SC: Whole-school environment supports learning.	HT	• In and Out Learning environment • Central resource • Class environment • ICT suite • Brain function implications for teaching	8500	• Learning styles • Teacher talk/Questioning • Multiple intelligences • Thinking skills • Reflection • Barriers to learning • Using other professionals	5000	• School-based research and enquiry • Using volunteers • Extending the learning day • Sharing best practices	5000
IO2: To develop an effective curriculum planning process. SC: Teachers plan confidently, using the new approach.	DHT	• Long-term plan • Medium/short • Planning files • Focus on foundation subjects	1100	• Focus on Numeracy and Literacy • High expectations • Include PSHE, key skills, homework • Evaluation of MTP and implications for future	500	• Creative approach to planning • Include SMSC	500
IO3: To establish a cycle for curriculum improvement over three years. SC: Detailed guidance for each area established.	DHT	• Science • ICT • PE • PSHE • Assessment (audit) • Early Years	5000	• English • Art • RE (KI5.3) • Geography • Spiritual dev (KI5.3b) • Assessment (good practice)	6000	• Maths • History • Music (KI5.2a) • DT • Moral • Cultural	6000
IO4: To enhance parental and community involvement with school. SC: Parents support events and express views. Increased links with community.	HT	• Annual questionnaire • Meetings with new parents • Lunchtime activities • Church group • Tuxfordian • HE links		• Policy for meetings • Improved communication • Links with 'Mine of Information' • Community use of ICT	1000	• Skills of parent partnership • Events to invite community into school	200

Improvement Area 4: Organisation and Leadership	Who?	Phased action areas to achieve strategy; indicative costs					
		2000–2001		2001–2002		2002–2003	
IO1: To develop holistic approach to school improvement planning. SC: Plan used and understood.	HT	• Involve staff and Governors • Plan to new rationale longer than one year • Monitoring and evaluation processes • Guidelines for Governors' visits	800	• Evaluate strategic plan • Involve children and parents • Reviews and evaluations feed into improvements • Plan drives budget • Evaluations used to inform improvements	50	• Evaluate strategic plan • Review strategic plan • Self-evaluation process • Undertake strategic analysis	50
IO2: To establish a shared leadership approach. SC: Subject Leaders take responsibility for subject development.	HT	• Job descriptions • Organised leader time • Curriculum budgets • Improvement files for targeted subjects	1000	• Improvement files for all subjects • Analysis of data • Resources • Role review • Professional development	5500	• Building teams • Policy • Review perceptions of leadership • Community of leaders, not just teachers	6000
IO3: To improve Governors' knowledge and understanding of school management and leadership. SC: Governors have increased confidence in their role.	HT	• Headteacher's report to link with improvement plan • Governors involved with INSET • Subcommittees • Reports for visits		• Induction programme • Policy for induction and training • Staff understanding of role	500		

Improvement Area 5: Staff	Who?	Phased action areas to achieve strategy; indicative costs		
		2000–2001	2001–2002	2002–2003
IO1: To improve the quality of learning and teaching through targeting professional learning to school and individual needs. SC: Individual and school needs are met. School a community of learners	HT	• NOF training • Professional library • Recording development opportunities • Staff meetings development focus 50	• NOF training • Professional library and focus on research articles • Joined up systems for PM/Prof development/SIP/M and E • Professional opportunities followed up with colleagues • Staff development and induction policy 4500 5500	• Use of research • Looking wider • Collaborative practice 6000
IO2: To improve the quality of learning through performance management. SC: Achievement of performance targets	HT	• Write policy • Implement process 1500	• Review cycle two • Review process 1500	• Include support staff, optional professional review 1750

5. Operational Plans: September 2001–August 2002

Improvement Area 1: Educational Standards	Governors' Responsibility: Strategic Development Committee (SDC) Pupils and Personnel Committee (PP)

Improvement Objective 1 Standards in English	Who? SL					

Success Criteria:
At least 80% of children in each class achieve their individual targets.

Key Actions	Who?	Resource Source	Time-scale	Monitoring When? Who? How?	Outcomes	Evaluation
a. To maintain realistic and challenging targets for each child in reading and writing, which are shared with the children	CT		Term 1 Term 2 Term 3	Term 2,3 SL Lit Gov	Records Wrk scrutiny Child disscn	Targets set in Sept, reviewed in Feb and evaluated in July	SLT then SDC
b. To establish target groups to support children in Years 1, 2, 3, 4	SL		Term 1	Term 2,3 Govs	Wrk scrutiny Records	Children make progress	SLT then SDC
c. To further develop school library and the use of class libraries	SL	£50 per curric area	Term 1	Term 2 Govs	Book review	Library more able to support curriculum	Literacy Gov then SDC
d. Update English policy	SL		Term 3	2002–03 SR	Observation	Policy evident in practice	SLT then SDC

Improvement Objective 2 Standards in Maths	Who? SL					

Success Criteria:
At least 80% of children in each class achieve their individual targets.

Key Actions	Who?	Resource Source	Time-scale	Monitoring When? Who? How?	Outcomes	Evaluation
a. Establish record system for maths	SL	SL time	Term 3	2002–03 HT	Discussion	Record system to support learning	SLT then SDC
b. To maintain the use of children's targets in maths	SL	SL time	Termly	Termly Govs	Work record scrutiny	Targets set in Sep, reviewed in Feb and evaluated in July	SLT then SDC
c. To establish target groups for potential high achievers in Year 6 and Year 2	CT	HT time	Term 1	Term 2 CT	Discussion	Able children access to weekly support	SLT then SDC

Improvement Objective 3
Children's attitudes towards school

Who? HT

Success *Criteria:*
Children are positive about school, are involved in events and take responsibility

Key Actions	Who?	Resource Source	Time-scale	Monitoring When? Who? How?		Outcomes	Evaluation
a. To develop policy for, and practice of, 'out of hours activities'	PE SL		Term 3	2001–02 HT	Observation	All follow policy when organising events	SLT then SDC
b. To develop children's whole-school responsibilities in school	HT		Term 1	Term 2 DHT	Observation	Children greater responsibility for our sch	SLT then SDC
c. To continue with School Council, enable children to contribute ideas (views about uniform, attendance, school impmt plan)	HT		Termly	Term 2 CT	Observation	Children positive about outcomes	SLT then SDC
d. To develop playground games used at lunchtime	PE SL	PSHE	Term 2	Term 3 HT	Observation Discussion	Children more able to play creatively	SLT then SDC

Improvement Objective 4
Behaviour

Who? HT

Success *Criteria:*
Consistency of staff response to children's behaviour

Key Actions	Who?	Resource Source	Time-scale	Monitoring When? Who? How?		Outcomes	Evaluation
a. To extend the use of circle time in all classes every week	HT	Staff library PSHE	Term 2	Term 3 KSC	Discussion	Circle time used to support self-esteem and right choices	SLT then SDC
b. To revise the behaviour code. To include rewards and sanctions	HT		Term 1	Term 2 KSC	Discussion	Policy seen in practice	SLT then PP
c. To develop a policy for anti-bullying	SENCo		Term 1	Term 2 HT	Discussion	Policy seen in practice	SLT then PP
d. To introduce, as necessary, a 'making the right choices' lunchtime club for invited participants	HT		Term 1	Term 2 SLT	Discussion	Less need for its existence	SLT then PP

Improvement Area 2:
Children

Governors' Responsibility: *Pupils and Personnel (PP)*

Improvement Objective 1
Attendance rates/incidents of lateness

Who? HT

Success Criteria:
Rate of attendance to be maintained at 94%. Incidence of lateness reduced by 10%.

Key Actions	Who?	Resource Source	Time-scale	Monitoring When? Who? How?		Outcomes	Evaluation
a. Attendance review of children identified last year to be maintained	Admin		Term 1, 2, 3	Termly HT	Data report	Parents informed of concerns. Achievement celebrated	SLT then PP
b. Review lateness each half term	Admin CT		Term 1, 2, 3	Termly HT	Data report	Parents informed of concerns. Achievement celebrated	SLT then PP
c. Continue to celebrate achievements	HT		Termly	Termly GvB ch	Observation HT report	Children's achievements celebrated	SLT then PP

Improvement Objective 2
SEN

Who? SENCo

Success Criteria:
Quality of SEN provision is impacting on children's activities and learning in all year groups.

Key Actions	Who?	Resource Source	Time-scale	Monitoring When? Who? How?		Outcomes	Evaluation
a. Establish guidelines for identifying 'able' children. Promote good learning strategies for potential high achievement	SENCo	SEN training budget	Term 2	Term 3 HT	Policy evident in practice	Plans show differentiated activities for able children	SLT then SDC
b. Update SEN policy and related policy into practice documents	SENCo		Term 1	Term 2 DHT	Policy evident in practice	Staff following procedures and policy	SLT then SDC
c. Develop staff expertise for teaching children with ASD needs	SENCo	PD time	Term 2	Term 3 DHT	Plans observation	Increased confidence in teaching children with complex needs	SLT then SDC
d. Teachers' planning directly linked to individual IEPs	SENCo		Term 1	Termly DHT	Plans observation	IEPs affect teaching and learning evident in reviews	SLT then SDC
e. To use data to investigate different groups, i.e. gender achievement			Term 1	Term 2 HT	Report	Identification of groups	SLT then PP
f. To write a policy for inclusion/equal opportunities	SENCo		Term 2	Term 3 KSC	Observation discussion	Equal opportunities seen in evidence	SLT then PP

Improvement Objective 3
School uniform

Who?
HT

Success Criteria:
At least 90% children consistently wearing school uniform.

Key Actions	Who?	Resource Source	Time-scale	Monitoring When? Who? How?		Outcomes	Evaluation
a. Spot checks and class awards	CT		Half termly	Half tmly HT	Scrutiny of class %	Increased commitment to uniform	SLT then PP
b. Letters home to request support from parents from non-compliants	HT		Termly	Termly CT	Observation	Increased support for school uniform	SLT then PP
c. Children to discuss desired changes to uniform in School Council	CT		Term 3	2002–03 HT	Observation	Increased commitment to uniform	SLT then PP

Improvement Area 3: **Quality of Education**	*Governors' Responsibility: Strategic Development Committee (SDC)*

Improvement Objective 1
Learning

Who?
HT

Success Criteria:
More effective learning throughout school.

Key Actions	Who?	Resource Source	Time-scale	Monitoring When? Who? How?		Outcomes	Evaluation
a. To establish an international link for each class teacher and each class	HT		Term 2	Term 3 SLT	Discussion	Teachers and children using e-mail	SLT then SDC
b. To continue to develop our understanding of learning; styles, multiple intelligs, emot intellig, brain gym, motivation, barriers to learning, thinking skills	HT	PD time	Termly	Term 3 SLT	Discussion Observation	Reflections affect practice	SLT then SDC
c. Write policy for learning and teaching	HT		Term 2	Term 3 Govs	Observation	Policy evident in practice	SLT then SDC
d. Maintain developments in learning environment	HT		Termly	Term1 Govs	Observation	Peer evaluation followed by school evaluation	SLT then SDC

Improvement Objective 2
Curriculum planning

	Who?
	DHT

Success Criteria:
Staff plan in a consistent way.
Subject leaders are able to use planning to monitor range and quality of curriculum.

Key Actions	Who?	Resource Source	Time-scale	Monitoring When? Who?	How?	Outcomes	Evaluation
a. Establish routine of LTP/MTP/STP	DHT		Term 2	Term 3 HT	Plans	Routine established and followed by all	SLT then SDC
b. Curriculum statement, policy and policy into practice written	DHT		Term 1	Term 2 KSC	Planning	Documents in place and in practice	SLT then SDC
c. Teachers able to use a variety of teaching strategies, i.e. questioning	DHT	PD time Reading	Term 3	2001–02 SL	Plans observation	Increased confidence in teaching strategies	SLT then SDC
d. MTP to include PSHE, key skills and homework	DHT		Term 3	2001–02 KSC	Plans	More comprehensive MTP	SLT then SDC

Improvement Objective 3
DT

	Who?
	SL

Success Criteria:
The quality of learning and teaching more effective throughout school.

Key Actions	Who?	Resource Source	Time-scale	Monitoring When? Who?	How?	Outcomes	Evaluation
a. Write a policy and long-term overview	SL		Term 2	Term 3 HT	Planning	Policy and overview used	SLT then SDC
b. Develop staff expertise and confidence in the subject	SL	PD time	Term 3	2002–03 DHT	Observation	Staff confident to teach subject	SLT then SDC
c. Audit, organise and maintain resources	SL		Term 1	Term 2 KSC	Discussion	Resources support learning and accessible	SLT then SDC
d. To promote the development of skills	SL	PD time	Term 3	2002–03 KSC	Observation Planning	Improved learning, improved progression	SLT then SDC
e. To ensure appropriate planning	SL		Term 2	Term 3 SL	Planning	Planning effective	SLT then SDC

Improvement Objective 4 Art — Who? SL

Success Criteria: Progression of skills and increased expectations evident throughout school.

Key Actions	Who?	Resource Source	Time-scale	Monitoring When? Who? How?	Outcomes	Evaluation
a. Write a policy and long-term overview for art and design	SL	PD time	Term 2	Term 3 HT / Planning	Reflected in planning	SLT then SDC
b. Develop staff expertise and confidence in the subject, workshops	SL	INSET PD time	Term 3	2002–03 DHT / Class observation	Effective teaching	SLT then SDC
c. Audit, organise and maintain resources	SL	Budget	Term 2	Term 3 KSC / Discussion	Resources organised, effective and evaluated	SLT then SDC
d. Introduce the use of sketchbooks throughout school	SL	Budget	Term 1	Term 2 KSC / Discussion	Every child to use sketchbooks Y1–Y6	SLT then SDC
e. To promote the development of skills	SL	SL time	Term 3	2002–03 SL / Observation	Staff understand and use skill development	SLT then SDC

Improvement Objective 5 Geography — Who? SL

Success Criteria: Development of skills evident throughout school.

Key Actions	Who?	Resource Source	Time-scale	Monitoring When? Who? How?	Outcomes	Evaluation
a. Write a policy and long-term overview	SL	PD time	Term 2	Term 3 HT / Planning	Policy and overview used	SLT then SDC
b. Develop staff expertise and confidence in the subject	SL	PD time	Term 3	2001–02 KSC / Observation	Staff confident to teach subject	SLT then SDC
c. Audit, organise and maintain resources	SL		Term 1	Term 2 KSC / Discussion	Resources support learning and accessible	SLT then SDC
d. To promote the development of geographical skills and thinking skills	SL	PD time	Term 3	2001–02 HT / Planning	Improved learning, improved progression	SLT then SDC
e. To use our international links in the teaching of geography	SL		Term 2	Term 3 KSC	Australia featured in Classes 1 and 5	SLT then SDC
f. To ensure appropriate planning	SL		Term 2	Term 3 SL / Planning	Planning effective	SLT then SDC

Improvement Objective 6   **Who?** HT
Parental involvement

Success Criteria:
Improved communication between school and parents.

Key Actions	Who?	Resource Source	Time-scale	Monitoring When? Who? How?		Outcomes	Evaluation
a. Policy and record for significant meetings	HT		Term 2	Term 3 KSC	Discussion	More effective communication	SLT then SDC
b. Annual questionnaire	HT		Term 2	Term 3 Govs	Report	Parents' views taken into consideration	SLT then SDC
c. Termly update on OFSTED action plan	HT		Termly	Term 2 Govs	Questionnaire	Parents kept up to date	SLT then SDC

Improvement Objective 7   **Who?** CC
Community involvement

Success Criteria:
Increased links between school and community.

Key Actions	Who?	Resource Source	Time-scale	Monitoring When? Who? How?		Outcomes	Evaluation
a. Members of community to be involved with lunchtime activities	HT		Term 1	Term 2 CC	Discussion	Lunchtime activity provided	SLT then PP
b. Regular school contributions to Parish Council paper and local papers	Gov		Termly	Termly CC	Newspapers	Community increased awareness of our achievements	SLT then PP
c. Make links with 'Mine of Information'	CC		Termly	Termly CC	Discussion	Increased awareness of community projects	SLT then PP
d. School represented on regeneration education forum	HT		Termly	Termly HT	Attendance	School involved in community projects	SLT then PP

Improvement Area 4: Organisation and Leadership	Governors' Responsibility: Strategic Development Committee (SDC), Pupils and Personnel (PP), Finance and General Purposes (FGP)

Improvement Objective 1
School improvement planning

Who?	HT

Success Criteria:
Plan used and understood by staff, Governors and children.

Key Actions	Who?	Resource Source	Time-scale	Monitoring When? Who? How?		Outcomes	Evaluation
a. Evaluate process, introduced last year	HT		Term 1	Term 1 SLT	Report	Improved process	SLT then SDC
b. Involve children in the process through School Council	HT		Term 2	Term 3 CT	Minutes	Children involved	SLT then PP
c. Planning drives budget, write next strategic plan/review and op plan	HT Fin Of	PD time	Term 3	2002–03 SDC	Minutes	Budget reflect priorities estabd through process	F&GP

Improvement Objective 2
Shared leadership

Who?	DHT

Success Criteria:
SLs take increasingly more responsibility for the development of their subjects/aspects.

Key Actions	Who?	Resource Source	Time-scale	Monitoring When? Who? How?		Outcomes	Evaluation
a. All subjects establish improvement file	SL		Term 2	Term 3 KSC	File	All improvements evidenced	SLT then SDC
b. SL skills further developed, i.e. analysis of data and understanding role of govs	HT	PD time	Term 3	2002–03 SLT	Discussion	Greater confidence	PP

Improvement Objective 3
Governors

Who?	Chair

Success Criteria:
Governors have increased confidence in their role.

Key Actions	Who?	Resource Source	Time-scale	Monitoring When? Who? How?		Outcomes	Evaluation
a. System for subcommittee agenda and procedures focus on SIP	HT		Term 2	Term 3 S-c chr	Obervation Discussion	Procedures understood and effective	Each sub-committee
b. Induction programme and documentation	DHT		Term 2	Term 3 Chair	Discussion	Role and practice understood	SDC
c. Annual plan of procedures	HT		Term 2	Term 3 Chair	Discussion	Plan to support 'a'	Sub-committees

Improvement Area 5: Staff	Governors' Responsibility: Pupils and Personnel (PP)

Improvement Objective 1
Professional learning

	Who? HT

Success Criteria:
Improved quality of learning and teaching through targeting professional learning to school needs and individual needs.

Key Actions	Who?	Resource Source	Time-scale	Monitoring When? Who? How?		Outcomes	Evaluation
a. Completion of NOF training	ICT SL		Term 2	Term 3 DHT	Observation Planning Discussion	Teachers confident and competent to teach ICT across subject areas	SLT then PP
b. Extend Professional Library	SL Lit		Term 1	Term 2 KSC	Discussion	Teachers have access to and use prof reading	SLT then PP
c. Establish process of joined thinking between PD, PM, SIP	HT		Term 3	2002–03 KSC	Observation Discussion	Process and record of effect established	SLT then PP
d. Information for supply teachers and record system established	HT		Term 1	Term 2 KSC	Observation Discussion	Information used and records useful	SLT then PP

Improvement Objective 2
Performance management

	Who? HT

Success Criteria:
Teachers achieve performance targets set at review.
Process supports improved quality of teaching.

Key Actions	Who?	Resource Source	Time-scale	Monitoring When? Who? How?		Outcomes	Evaluation
a. Implement cycle two	HT	Budget	Term 1	Term 2 Govs	Discussion	Performance review completed and targets set, policy followed	SLT then PP
b. Review process and policy	DHT		Term 3	Termly Govs	Discussion	Process supports improvement	SLT then PP

6. Headteacher's Report for Governors: Summer Term 2002

1. Educational Standards

1.1 /1.2 Pupil achievement
Year 6 Task and Test Results (School data)
Achievements towards the targets set for 2002 (set 2000)
Year 2 Task and Test Results
Children's individual targets

1.1 Standards in English
d. Policy

1.2 Standards in maths
a. Record system for maths

1.3 Attitudes to learning
a. Policy for out-of-hours activities
c. School Council meeting

1.4 Behaviour and values
a. School behaviour code and the use of circle time

End of term awards:

- Friendship tree award for getting the most leaves on the Friendship tree this term
- Attendance awards for the term and the year
- Completed achievement sticker chart.

2. Children

2.1 Attendance
a. Attendance
b. Lateness
c. Celebrations

2.2 Uniform
a. Class awards
b. Letters home
c. School Council suggestions

2.3 Special Educational Needs
a/f Guidelines for high achievement and inclusion this term

3. *Quality of Education*

3.1 Learning
a. International links
b. Use of brain gym/developing thinking skills
c. Environment

3.2 Curriculum planning
c. Use of teaching strategies
d. Medium-term plans

3.3 DT
b. Staff expertise
d. Development of skills

3.6 Art
b. Staff expertise
e. Development of skills

3.5 Geography
b. Staff expertise
d. Development of skills/ thinking

3.6 Parental involvement
c. OFSTED action plan

3.7 Community Involvement
b. Parish newspaper
c. 'Mine of Information' links
d. Education forum

3.8 Visits and visitors

3.9 Special events

4. *Organisation and Leadership*

4.1 School Improvement Plan
c. Next steps

4.2 Shared Leadership
b. SL skills

Subject Leadership

What?		Leader	Days of non-class time	
	Year of SIP focus		Per year	Term 3

4.3 Governors
Governors' focused visits

2001–2002	Focus	When?	Governors?	Staff link
Autumn term	Art			
	English			
Spring term	Environment			
	Behaviour			
Summer term	Geography			
	DT			

5. Staff
5.1 Professional learning
b. The Professional library
c. Process

INSET days
Individual opportunities

Who?	What?	Time?

Staff appointments
Staff welfare
Absences Summer Term

S   –sickness
LA –leave of absence: key of reasons: G = graduation; F = funeral
      (others added here as needed)

Who?	S	LA		S	LA		S	LA

Staff absence management: running total April 2002 – March 2003

5.2 Performance management
b. Process review

Chapter 7

Secondary school planning case study

Ray Watkin

In this chapter, we provide a case example of a secondary school which has based its approach to school planning on our model. We are very pleased that Ray Watkin, headteacher, and the staff and governors of Whitley Abbey Community School have found our model useful and have adapted it to meet their own unique needs. We are grateful to be given their permission to use it here.

The school's plan is based on the following timescales shown in Figure 7.1

The document is presented in five parts:

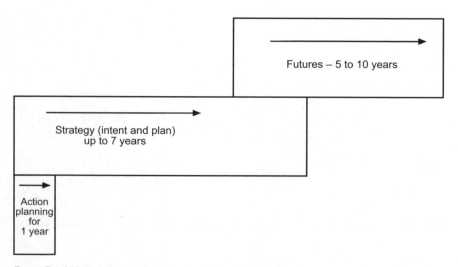

Figure 7.1 Whitley Abbey Community School timescales

1. Introduction – which explains the context in which the document was developed.
2. A futures perspective on Whitley Abbey Community School – which sets out the future challenges and gives some indication of the school's intended response to the futures issues.
3. The strategic intent framework for the school – which lists five intents and sets out the capability measures which the school intends to use in pursuit of its intents.
4. The Strategic Plan for the school – which is structured into four strategic areas to be achieved over a three-year period.
5. The Annual Development Plan which comprises targets, followed by the responses to these of the senior leadership group (SLG), the curriculum areas and the pastoral teams. For reasons of space, we have included only some of the SLG responses (one for each area) and the responses of one curriculum area and one pastoral team.

Towards 2012: A planning framework for Whitley Abbey Community School

1. Introduction

Towards 2010 was written by the headteacher and presented to governors and staff with a curriculum and pastoral management responsibility as a draft document in September 2000. The intention was to set up a staff/governors working group to review the draft and publish as an agreed futures framework.

The move into the new school building in September 2000 and the associated issues meant that it wasn't until January 2002 that a working group of governors considered the framework and found the document complex. However, the School Leadership Group (SLG) drew on *Towards 2010* to identify priorities, targets and individual responsibilities in drawing up year-on-year plans. In 2000/01 it was called the Operational Target Setting Plan. From 2001/02 the document was called the Annual Development Plan (ADP). SLG reviewed the *Towards 2010* framework at the end of the summer term 2002. *Towards 2012* is the result of the review.

The plans for the future of the school reflect its Statement of Philosophy:

> *As a comprehensive school, we value all members of our community as individual people with differing needs and abilities. We are working to provide a stimulating and caring environment, in which everybody thrives.*

and its Core Purpose:

> *To ensure that the professional activities of the school are harnessed to enable every young person to learn effectively so that their highest potential is achieved.*

2. A futures perspective on Whitley Abbey Community School

Futures thinking, by its very nature, is uncertain. It is clear that employment patterns are changing rapidly with an emphasis on knowledge-based work. We are living through a period where information, communication and bio-technologies are developing at an unprecedented rate. Economic activity is becoming increasingly global. This globalisation, supported by the new technologies, is having a profound effect on political activity at the national and international levels. Will we ever adopt the euro? This turbulence is also a feature of local politics and activity, driven by government requirements.

Making sense of this whirlwind of change is no easy task. We have identified three futures aspects, which map onto our Statement of Philosophy and Core Purpose. These three are:

> 1) *'Anytime – anywhere' learning will become part of a person's lifestyle from childhood through to old age.*
>
> 2) *Curriculum will be defined in terms of processes, skills and competencies developed through areas of learning and knowledge themes.*
>
> 3) *Whitley Abbey will be a facilitator of life-long learning for the people in the community it serves.*

The following maps out what we believe could be the potential impact of these futures aspects and identifies how the school will respond:

Future Aspect 1: 'Anytime – anywhere' learning will become part of a person's lifestyle from childhood through to old age.

	Potential impact on the school		School response
a)	Young people must be able to access their curriculum and school resources at any time during the day, every day.	i)	The school must ensure the means for all pupils and their families to access the school's intranet.
b)	Pupils and parents must be able to access the teachers' views on progress, what needs to be done to improve, where pupils stand in relation to personal achievement and achievement against bench-marked standards.	i)	Pupils and parents must be able to access assessment and help information at any time.
c)	Adults in the community should be able to access the school's curriculum to enable themselves to enlarge their personal achievements portfolio.	i)	School must be able to support life-long learning.
d)	Enable 'anytime – anywhere' assessment to achievement.	i)	The school must ensure the means for all community members to record their achievements at any time.

Future Aspect 2: *Curriculum will be defined in terms of processes, skills and competencies developed through areas of learning and knowledge themes.*

Potential impact on the school		School response	
a)	Pupils will negotiate their individual learning plan, setting targets for personal learning and development based on their individual learning styles and developing aspirations.	i)	The establishment of a personal tutor for each pupil and the development of a mentoring network involving both school based and external mentors.
		ii)	The development of curriculum experiences which ensure all pupils become effective learners so that they achieve their highest potential.
b)	Changes to the role of the teacher.	i)	Support teachers in the development of their understanding of individual learning styles and research into the neurological basis of learning.
		ii)	Carefully planned in-service development and the establishment of collaborative networks both within and outside of school to support teachers in their new roles.
c)	Flexibility will have to be a feature of school organisation to accommodate individual pupil needs and the needs of the community.	i)	A different approach to school timetabling to allow for individual learning plans.
		ii)	A different approach to conditions of service and staffing allowing for flexibility, time off in lieu so that the needs of pupils and the community can be accommodated.
		iii)	The employment of support staff to enable the school facilities to be used between 8 a.m. and 10 p.m., 6 days a week, 52 weeks a year (?).

Future Aspect 3: *Whitley Abbey will be a facilitator of life-long learning for the people in the community it serves.*

Potential impact on the school	School response
a) School will have to work in close partnership with all other education providers in the community catchment area.	i) The establishment of a community life long learning forum. ii) The establishment of a community intranet.
b) The school will have to establish a multi-agency approach in partnership with the contributing agencies to ensure the needs of all the members of the catchment community can be addressed.	i) To be a key player in the establishment of a multi-agency framework involving health, social services, the police, the youth justice service (etc.). ii) To build multi-agency involvement in the school organisation framework including timetabling professional meeting time.
c) Changes to the leadership and management responsibilities in the school.	i) Leadership and management responsibilities will be redefined and new personnel appointed to ensure the school effectively discharges its community role and attendant responsibilities.
d) A change to the funding framework to the overall school budget to reflect the enhanced role in the community.	i) To support staff responsible for school finance in accommodating these wider duties including the appointment of additional personnel if necessary.
e) The home-school partnership will be redefined.	i) To develop ways of engaging all families in the core business of the school. ii) To enable parents to have real influence on the core business of the school. iii) To ensure pupils have real influence on the core business of the school.

3. The strategic intent framework for Whitley Abbey Community School

In order to move Whitley Abbey to a position where it can engage with the futures aspects set out in Section 2 it will be necessary to build the capability in the school so that performance and process are in line with these new demands. This strategic intent framework identifies five strategic intents:

1. To establish 'anytime – anywhere' learning for all pupils using the power and connectivity of ICT.
2. To develop a leadership culture throughout the school.
3. To link home, community primary schools and other learning providers with Whitley Abbey to develop a learning community.
4. To build flexibility into school organisation and ways of working.
5. To achieve specialist college status.

The framework sets out the strategic intents and identifies the capability-building measures which will be employed to achieve them over the next 3 to 7 years. As the school measures progress towards these intents (see checkpoint dates in column 2 below) then it will become clear whether the intent is achievable within the context of the strategic plan (Section 4) or will have to be reformulated. In this way unforeseen events, new requirements and changes which directly affect the school, can be accommodated and the strategic intent framework and Strategic Plan adjusted accordingly.

Intent 1: To establish 'anytime – anywhere' learning using the power and connectivity of ICT.

Capability building measures	Move to strategic plan or Reformulate intent
i) Investigate schemes to provide laptop computers for all pupils ii) Develop a culture where all staff integrate ICT in their teaching. iii) Investigate sponsorship and support. iv) Investigate means of validating out-of-school learning experiences. v) Establish a time period for activities and review relationship to strategic plan.	*Check in June 2004* *Either* The capability will be established and there will be a clear understanding of how 'anytime – anywhere' learning can be progressed to strategic plans. *Or* Capability measures will be reframed to enable the intent to progress to strategic plan.

Intent 2: To develop a leadership culture throughout the school.

Capability building measures	Move to strategic plan or Reformulate intent
i) Support staff in moving towards their new roles in the staffing structure through collaborative networks. ii) Provide leadership and management development for all staff. iii) Develop a culture where staff experiment and try new approaches to teaching and learning and pupil support. iv) Develop the leadership and management capabilities to work with other agencies to support the Statement of Philosophy and Core Purpose. v) Establish a time period for activities and review relationship to strategic plan.	*Check in June 2004* *Either* Capabilities will be established and an in-depth understanding of leadership in relation to roles and responsibilities will be present, enabling this intent to be part of strategic planning. *Or* Capability measures will be reframed to enable the intent to progress to strategic plans.

Intent 3: To link home, community primary schools and other learning providers with Whitley Abbey to develop a learning community.

Capability building measures	Move to strategic plan or Reformulate intent
i) Investigate the latest developments in establishing community intranet capabilities.	*Check in June 2004* *Either*
ii) Identify and engage other learning providers in the community.	Capabilities will be established and partnerships forged to enable this intent to be part of the strategic
iii) Communicate the concept of a learning community to Community Primary Schools and other learning providers.	planning process. *Or*
iv) Investigate resource support for the initiative via LEA and other potential partners.	Capability measure will be reframed to engage the community in developing the understanding and potential to move towards a learning community.
v) Develop a culture where community inter-relationships are at the heart of the school's core purpose.	
vi) Investigate the most appropriate ways to support community inter-relationships through the leadership structure of the school.	
vii) To develop a culture where parents become fully involved in all aspects of school as equal partners.	
viii) Establish a time period for activities and review relationships to the strategic plan.	

Intent 4: To build flexibility into school organisation and ways of working.

Capability building measures	Move to strategic plan or Reformulate intent
i) Investigate alternative approaches to school timetabling.	*By June 2004 (or sooner)*
	Either
ii) Investigate what flexibility can be achieved in relation to teachers' conditions of service.	The capabilities will be established and a clear understanding of the issues around flexibility achieved so that this
iii) Establish a forum for exploring flexibility to include teachers, governors, unions, LEA and other interested community partners.	intent can become part of the strategic planning process.
	Or
iv) Develop the organisation to enable the community to access school facilities from 8.00 a.m. to 10.00 p.m., 7 days (?) a week, 52 weeks (?) a year.	Capability measures will be reframed to enable an understanding of what is possible in terms of flexibility to move towards this intent via the strategic planning process.
v) Understand and include the financial implications of extensive community use of the school.	
vi) Establish a time period for activities and review relationships.	

Intent 5: To achieve specialist college status.

Capability building measures	Move to strategic plan or Reformulate intent
i) Achieve a balanced budget position.	*Check in June 2004* *Either*
ii) With school and LEA, develop agreed approach to specialist college status.	The capabilities will be established and a clear understanding of the application process for specialist
iii) To identify sponsorship partners and resource support.	college status achieved so that this becomes part of the strategic planning process.
iv) To develop the capacity to respond quickly to the resource bidding process with DfES, LEA and other potential sources of income and sponsorship.	*Or* Capability measures will be reframed to enable the understanding of the specialist school application process to progress to the strategic planning process.

4. The strategic plan for Whitley Abbey Community School

The strategic plan has four Strategic Areas which map onto the school's Statement of Philosophy and its Core Purpose and also onto the futures perspective and the strategic intent framework shown above.

The Strategic Areas are:

1. Quality of Learning and Teaching.
2. Physical and financial management arrangements.
3. Structural and organisational management.
4. Community inter-relationships.

The plans to achieve targets in each strategic area are shown below with dates at which progress will be reviewed and, if necessary, plans will be modified.

Strategic Area 1:   *Quality of Learning and Teaching.*

Strategic targets	Time frame	Resource implications	
a) To improve the levels of literacy throughout the school so that 70% of pupils reach Level 5 by Year 9 and all pupils achieve an appropriate accreditation in English language in Year 11.	*Review in June 2004*	i)	Whole-school in-service on KS3 National Strategy in Literacy.
		ii)	Support for Literacy Steering Group.
		iii)	Meeting time and printing costs for schemes of work.
b) To improve the levels of numeracy throughout the school so that over 70% of pupils reach Level 5 by Year 9 and all pupils achieve an appropriate accreditation in numeracy in Year 11.	*Review in 2004*	i)	Whole-school in-service on KS3 National Strategy in Numeracy.
		ii)	Support for Numeracy Steering Group.
		iii)	Meeting time and printing costs for schemes of work.
c) To develop a whole-school learning policy.	*Review in 2004*	i)	Support for Learning Policy implementation.
d) To develop a pupil self-evaluation framework with respect to personal targets, learning achievements, and the reviewing of the quality of teaching.	*Review in 2004*	i)	Identification and installation of software to support self-evaluation.
e) To ensure all staff integrate ICT in their teaching and assessment activities.	*Review in 2004*	i)	Improve access to computers via teacher laptops and PCs
		ii)	Identification and installation of software to support teacher assessment and planning.
f) To improve the quality of teaching throughout the school using the monitoring framework and OFSTED criteria so that all lessons observed are satisfactory or better.	*Review in 2004*	i)	Training for Curriculum Leaders and Pastoral Leaders in the use of monitoring instruments to assess quality of teaching.
		ii)	Time allocated for observations and review.

Strategic Area 2:   *Physical and financial management arrangements.*

	Strategic targets	Time frame		Resource implications
a)	Build up the school ICT capability to deliver the school ICT vision within the LEA ICT development plan.	*Review in 2004*	i)	Annual running costs for ICT – including Broadband and hardware replacement and software development.
b)	To install the wireless infra-structure to enable the development of 'anytime – anywhere' learning using laptop computers.	*Review 2004*	i)	Funding for laptops for staff and pupils.
			ii)	Support for work with governors and parents to roll out a laptop rent/purchase scheme.
c)	To achieve a year-on-year balanced budget.	*Review annually*	i)	Support for work to identify and secure sponsorship (additional funding).

Strategic Area 3:   *Structural and organisational management.*

	Strategic targets	Time frame		Resource implications
a)	To ensure all staff with a leadership responsibility are involved in individual and collaborative in-service activities in relation to their leadership and management roles.	*Review in 2004*	i)	In-service training costs to support leadership and management development.
b)	To review all school policies to develop a coherent and responsive framework.	*Review in 2004*	i)	Support for the Governors Anti-Racist Policy Working Group.
			ii)	Support for policy development.
c)	To develop a timetabling framework with the flexibility to accommodate independent learning approaches.	*Review in 2004*	i)	Support for a working group to investigate school timetabling.

Strategic Area 4: *Community inter-relationships.*

Strategic targets	Time frame	Resource implications
a) To work with our community Primary Schools to develop cross-phase learning activities and to support Year 6 to Year 7 progression.	*Review in 2004*	i) Support for headteacher engagement in the learning and progression aspirations of target 1. ii) Support for cross-phase development.
b) To develop a home–school partnership framework to include all families.	*Review in 2004*	i) Support for consultant work to survey parental views. ii) Support for multi-agency approach to engage all families.
c) To develop a Whitley Abbey Community and Partner Schools Intranet.	*Review in 2004*	i) Support for the Riverside Intranet. ii) Support for a community primary school intranet.

5. The Annual Development Plan

The Annual Development Plan supports the school's Statement of Philosophy and Core Purpose. The plan's targets are organised into the four strategic areas which, through the relationship with the Strategic Plan, support the futures framework as set out above.

The section which follows shows:

1. Overall Annual Development Plan (ADP) targets for the academic year.
2. The Senior Leadership Group's ADP in response to the overall targets.
3. Curriculum area ADPs in response to overall targets highlighted for attention in the academic year plus specific curriculum area targets.
4. Pastoral teams ADPs in response to overall targets highlighted for attention in the academic year plus specific pastoral team targets.

N.B.

All ADPs are put together for the first Finance and Strategic Planning subcommittee meeting of the governing body which is held in October.

The ADPs are reviewed by the Senior Leadership Group, Curriculum Leaders and Pastoral Leaders by the end of June in the academic year so that the next year's ADP whole-school targets can be developed.

In relation to parts 2, 3 and 4 above, we have only shown examples as follows:

- *targets A1, B4, C2 and D3 from the Senior team's response to the overall ADP*
- *the plans from the Expressive Art curriculum area (A1, 2, 3, and C1 are the only ones required at this level)*
- *the plans from the Year 10 pastoral team.*

Whitley Abbey Community School
Overall Annual Development Plan (ADP) Targets for 2002/03

Statement of Philosophy

As a comprehensive school, we value all members of our community as individual people with differing needs and abilities. We are working to provide a stimulating and caring environment, in which everybody thrives.

Core Purpose

To ensure that the professional activities of the school are harnessed to enable every young person to learn effectively so that their highest potential is achieved.

Strategic Area A) Quality of Learning and Teaching		Strategic Area B) Physical and financial management arrangements		Strategic Area C) Stuctural and organisational management		Strategic Area D) Community inter-relationships	
1) * To improve our teaching and learning styles so that pupil performance is enhanced through their engagement with their own learning.		1) To ensure an in-year balance is achieved for the financial year 2002/03.	ATi	1) * To ensure team handbooks are reviewed and amended in relation to current school policies.		1) To progress multi-agency work to ensure all young people thrive.	VWr
2) * To develop our capabilities to use assessment data to inform planning and use the information to engage and inform pupils with respect to their individual progress.		2) To put in place arrangements to ensure subsequent years achieve an in-year balance.	ATi	2) To develop a programme for the ongoing review of school policies against our duties with respect to the Anti-Racist Policy.	ACI	2) To undertake research into parental views and wishes to inform future action.	RWa
3) * To ensure schemes of work exist as medium-term planning tools to address our responsibilities with respect to literacy, numeracy, ICT, citizenship, anti-racist strategies and equal opportunities.		3) To progress development of MARA House and the Learning Development Centre.	VWr	3) To develop a programme for the ongoing review and revision of school job descriptions.	RW/ATi	3) To create a framework to facilitate continuity and progression between Key Stages 2 and 3 with our community primary schools.	RWa
		4) With governors, to prioritise and progress building issues.	RWa /ATi	4) To review the management of staff cover arrangements to inform the way forward for 2003/04.	EBr		
		5) To develop our capacity to exploit external funding possibilities.	RWa				

(Whole-school targets: * indicates targets which will be addressed in team development plans.)

Whitley Abbey Community School
Senior Leadership Group Annual Development Plan 2002/03

A1) To improve our teaching and learning styles so that pupil performance is enhanced through their engagement with their own learning.

Action/tasks and strategies	Who responsible	Resources	Start and end dates	Success criteria	Review and evaluation by	Evidence
Differentiation						
1) To evaluate schemes of work and supporting materials at KS3.	Curriculum Leaders Curriculum teams Citizenship group	Training days Meeting time Directed time SAS/NS consultants QCA guidance	2 per term Sept to July	i) 6 plus unit schemes to meet minimum requirements	SLG Line Manager. Class/PLs and teams. SAS/ Consultants	
2) To focus on a minimum of two units of work in each of Years 7, 8 and 9.						
National Strategy Implementation						
1) To use the framework to review teaching and learning styles at KS3.	Curriculum Leaders Curriculum teams Citizenship groups	Training days Meeting time Directed time SAS/NS consultants QCA guidance Whole-year work review Y8	Evaluation of team teaching & learning styles by Dec 02. Moderation observation meetings. Teaching & Learning policy by Easter 03.	i) Evidence of National Strategy in Schemes. ii) Moderation discussion in minutes. iii) Year 8 work review completed.	SLG Line Manager Class/Pastoral Leaders and teams SAS/ Consultants	

Capability to analyse and respond to student behaviour needs					
1) To use peer review, monitoring of referral forms and Department responses and Pastoral review of cohort performance to inform and enhance staff capability.	Curriculum/Pastoral Leaders Pastoral teams Curriculum teams SLG	Meeting time Directed time Referral pro forma Peer review training External agency involvement – BSS LSU liaison with teams	Ongoing	i) Reduction in use of internal exclusion. ii) Appropriate use of referral form for School Action planning. Reduction in fixed term exclusion.	SLG weekly monitoring. ACI spot checks each half term. CL/PL weekly process review
Teaching and Learning Policy					
1) To create a learning policy that reflects current pedagogical knowledge.	SLG/JLG Pastoral/Curriculum teams	Meeting agenda time	Formulate draft whole-school policy – Dec 02.	i) Whole-school policy in place and curriculum/PSHE-specific policies/ organisational responses in team handbooks.	JLG SLG line management
2) To create department policies requiring area-specific approaches.			Department policy/response – Easter 03.		Curriculum Leaders
3) To involve teams in exploring new strategies, evaluating current practice.			Confirm whole-school and department approach – July 02.		Citizenship Group SAS/ Consultants

continued …

A1) continued

Action/tasks and strategies	Who responsible	Resources	Start and end dates	Success criteria	Review and evaluation by	Evidence
Team self-review – OFSTED framework.						
1) To create team capacity to self-review in terms of: observation (line and peer based), moderation of outcomes and review of schemes of work.	Curriculum/Pastoral Leaders Pastoral teams Curriculum teams SLG	Training days Meeting time Directed time SAS/Consultants OFSTED handbook	As required through other strand start/end times. By Dec 02.	i) Evidence of meeting time for self-review ii) Evidence of observation and moderation.	SLG line manager. Class/PLs and teams.	
2) To support the above strands through this process			Spring term	iii) Rewriting of team leader job descriptions to steer this whole year group work review.		

B4) With Governors to prioritise and progress building issues.

Action/tasks and strategies	Who responsible	Resources	Start and end dates	Success criteria	Review and evaluation by	Evidence
1) Snagging and design issues lists merged and categorised by status and costs.	RWa, ATi	Meeting time Review time	Sept 02	i) Spreadsheet produced	SLG	
2) Issues prioritised for governor approval and built into the school asset management plan.	RWa, ATi	Meeting time Premises sub-committee time Secretarial support	Oct 02 Oct 02	i) Priority list produced ii) Premises sub approves priorities	SLG Premises sub	
3) Programme for 2002/03 approved by governors and put into action.	RWa, ATi	Full governors meeting	Nov 02 By Sept 02	i) Programme approved ii) Priority issues dealt with	Premises sub	
4) To involve pupils & staff in identifying building and grounds issues for future action.	SLG School Council	Meeting time & resourcing investigation work with staff & pupils	During 2002/03	i) Process established to access staff and pupils' views	SLG Premises sub	

C2) To develop a programme for the ongoing review of school policies against our duties with respect to Anti-Racist Policy.

Action/tasks and strategies	Who responsible	Resources	Start and end dates	Success criteria	Review and evaluation by	Evidence
1) To present the Anti-Racist policy to all staff and explore understanding of the core intent.	ACI Governor working group	Staff meeting time with all staff – teaching and support.	Oct half term to Dec 02	i) Staff meeting recorded. ii) Team handbooks to include a team response to the whole-school policy. Schemes of work to include evidence of anti-racist strategy planning.	Governor working group	
2) To involve all in developing an implementation strategy.	ACI Governor working group SLG JLG	Open meetings. Governor subcomm. time	Oct half term. Other meetings as in calendar and as plan (to be created) dictates.	i) Strategy in place.	Governor working group	
3) To formulate this strategy and a policy review mechanism for all school policies through the Governors' Anti-Racist working group.	ACI Governor subcommittee Governing body subcommittee	Governor time Agenda time on meetings	By Dec 02 By Feb 03	i) Policy review timescale in place. ii) At least one key policy reviewed to evaluate the process.	Governor working group	

4) To inform the current/ future School Development Plan in light of any urgent issues identified through the above.	ACI	Meeting time	By July 03	i) Evidence of a strategic response in the ADP review process 02/03.	Full governing body June 02
5) To progress the Collective Worship policy in relation to the outcomes of the staff consultation.	Collective worship working group RWa	Meeting time and implementation costs	By Oct 02	i) Collective worship co-ordinator appointed.	SLG
			By Oct 02	ii) Working group established.	SLG
			From Jan 03	iii) Pilot implemented.	SLG Curriculum sub

D3) To create a framework to facilitate continuity and progression between Key Stages 2 and 3 with our community primary schools.

Action/tasks and strategies	Who responsible	Resources	Start and end dates	Success criteria	Review and evaluation by	Evidence
1) To explore the concept of a learning community with community primary school headteachers and develop a strategic approach to support its realisation.	RWa	Meeting time Visiting time Hospitality costs Secretarial support	Sept 2002 to July 2003 By Easter 2003	i) Regular meetings with community primary school headteachers established ii) Strategic approach agreed.	SLG SLG	
2) With community primary school headteachers, to develop a framework to support Key Stage 2 to Key Stage 3 transition.	RWa, DHa, VWr	Meeting time Visiting time Hospitality costs Secretarial support	By Easter 2003	i) Framework developed.	SLG Curriculum sub	
3) With community primary school headteachers, to consider ways of developing cross-phase learning activities in a range of curriculum areas.	RWa, DHa, VWr Curriculum Leaders	Meeting time Visiting time Hospitality costs Secretarial support	During 2002/03	i) Curriculum areas identified and learning activities initiated.	SLG Headteachers Curriculum sub	

Whitley Abbey Community School
Creative Art Development Plan 2002/03

A1) To improve our teaching and learning styles so that pupil performace is enhanced through their engagement with their own learning.

Action/tasks and strategies	Who responsible	Resources	Start and end dates	Success criteria	Review and evaluation by	Evidence
i) Improve teaching styles within, will enhance pupils' understanding of the expressive arts through:						
a) A thematic cross-curricular approach for Year 7 & 8 pupils	KTo HVo CBu ASd MMa	Meeting time Collection Visual Resources (LRC)	Year 7: Oct 02 – Jan 03 Year 8: Jan 03 – Mar 03 Year 9: Mar 03 – Jul 03	i) 3 P.O.S. planned. ii) Pupil evaluations. iii) Staff evaluation through staff discussion and minuted. iv) Visual/Audio record of pupils' work.	KTo HVo CBu	
b) A combined expressive Arts project for Year 9 pupils. Develop & deliver a combined P.O.S. for each year group within KS3, paying particular attention to differentiation & supporting materials.	AEI					

continued…

A1) continued

Action/tasks and strategies	Who responsible	Resources	Start and end dates	Success criteria	Review and evaluation by	Evidence
ii) Review and revise departmental policy documents in line with current school policy, to include a learning policy for each department.	KTo HVo CBu	Meeting time Directed time Whole-school policy approach	Oct 2002 – Easter 2003	i) Learning policy in place. ii) Deparmental policy documents revised and in place.	HVo CBu KTo EBr	
iii) For all teaching staff to become familiar with the National Strategy Framework, for this to be reflected in revised S.O.W. and evident in teaching styles. Monitored through peers/line management observations.	KTo HVo CBu ASd MMa NSa	Meeting time Directed time N.S. guidance	Oct 2002	i) Revised S.O.W. ii) Reduction in use of I.E.	KTo HVo CBu EBr	

Future Consideration/Planning Notes

Key
√ =Complete; (√) = Completed, to be confirmed in September; **P** = Partial; **X** = Not done

A2) To develop our capabilities to use assessment data to inform planning and use the information to engage and inform pupils with respect to their individual progress.

Action/tasks and strategies	Who responsible	Resources	Start and end dates	Success criteria	Review and evaluation by	Evidence
i) Establish departmental databases to monitor and record progress of individual pupils.	KTo CBu HVo ASd MMa NSa	Directed time Software Pupil data	Oct 2002 – Dec 2002	i) Databases in use across Expressive Arts.	KTo HVo CBu EBr	
ii) Establish target-setting mechanisms on a departmental basis with Expressive Art overview.	KTo CBu HVo	Meeting time Directed time Pupil data	Oct 02 – Jul 03	i) Students aware of targets. ii) Students make expected or better progress.	KTo HVo CBu RBr	

Future Consideration/Planning Notes

Key
√ =Complete; (√) = Completed, to be confirmed in September; **P** = Partial; **X** = Not done

A3) To ensure schemes of work exist as medium-term planning tools to address our responsibilities with respect to literacy, numeracy, ICT, citizenship, anti-racist strategies and equal opportunities.

Action/tasks and strategies	Who responsible	Resources	Start and end dates	Success criteria	Review and evaluation by	Evidence
i) Review schemes of work in line with National Strategy guidance.	KTo CBu HVo	Meeting time Directed time National Strategy guidance	Oct 2002 – July 2003	i) Reviewed schemes of work.	KTo EBr	
ii) Use Whitley Abbey proforma to plan/revise S.O.W. with respect to Target A3 including G and T, spirituality. Minimum 2 per year in Years 7, 8 and 9.	KTo CBu HVo	Meeting time Directed time Proforma agreed by SLG	Oct 2002 – July 2003	i) Schemes of work in place, delivered and evaluated.	KTo HVo CBu EBr	

Future Consideration/Planning Notes

Key
√ =Complete; (√) = Completed, to be confirmed in September; **P** = Partial; **X** = Not done

C1) To ensure team handbooks are reviewed and amended in relation to current school policies.

Action/tasks and strategies	Who responsible	Resources	Start and end dates	Success criteria	Review and evaluation by	Evidence
i) Review and revise departmental handbooks for Music, Drama and Art in line with SLG guidelines.	KTo HVo CBu	Meeting time Directed time	Oct 2002 – Easter 2003	i) Handbooks completed and in place.	KTo EBr	
ii) Create an Expressive Arts team introduction for inclusion in all 3 handbooks.	KTo	Time	Oct 2002 – Easter 2003	i) Introduction completed and in place.	EBr	

Future Consideration/Planning Notes

Key
√ =Complete; (√) = Completed, to be confirmed in September; **P** = Partial; **X** = Not done

Whitley Abbey Community School
Year 10 Development Plan 2002/03

A1) To improve our teaching and learning styles so that pupil performace is enhanced through their engagement with their own learning.

Action/tasks and strategies	Who responsible	Resources	Start and end dates	Success criteria	Review and evaluation by	Evidence
i) Develop a variety of teaching and learning styles within PSHE delivery.	DHa AEl Tutors	Meeting time Resources Training	Oct 2002 – July 2003	i) No pupils sent to internal exclusion from tutor period.	VWr	i.e. records

Future Consideration/Planning Notes

Key
√ =Complete; (√) = Completed, to be confirmed in September; **P** = Partial; **X** = Not done

A2) To develop our capabilities to use assessment data to inform planning and use the information to engage and inform pupils with respect to their individual progress.

Action/tasks and strategies	Who responsible	Resources	Start and end dates	Success criteria	Review and evaluation by	Evidence
i) Introduce individual target setting.	DHa Tutors	Curriculum time Reprographics Meeting Time	Oct 2002 – Jan 2003	i) All pupils have targets by February half term.	VWr	Tutor/pupil files

Future Consideration/Planning Notes

A3) To ensure schemes of work exist as medium-term planning tools to address our responsibilities with respect to literacy, numeracy, ICT, citizenship, anti-racist strategies and equal opportunities.

Action/tasks and strategies	Who responsible	Resources	Start and end dates	Success criteria	Review and evaluation by	Evidence
i) Develop PSHE teaching and learning policy.	DHa AEI	Meeting time	Nov 2002 – June 2003	i) Policy in place by Sept 03.	VWr	
ii) Self-review PSHE time.	DHa Pastoral team	Evaluation sheets Meeting time	Nov 2002 onwards	i) Termly evaluation sheets completed.	VWr	Evaluation sheets check by DHa/VWr.

Future Consideration/Planning Notes

i) Both actions will begin following whole-school actions
ii)

Key
√ =Complete; (√) = Completed, to be confirmed in September; **P** = Partial; **X** = Not done

C1) To ensure team handbooks are reviewed and amended in relation to current school policies.

Action/tasks and strategies	Who responsible	Resources	Start and end dates	Success criteria	Review and evaluation by	Evidence
i) Year team handbook produced.	DHa	Time Reprographics	Oct 2002 – Ongoing	i) In place by Sept 03.	VWr	

Future Consideration/Planning Notes

Key
√ =Complete; (√) = Completed, to be confirmed in September; **P** = Partial; **X** = Not done

Chapter 8

LEA case study

Angela Jensen

Introduction

This chapter includes an example of the way in which an LEA has presented our ideas for use in schools of all types. We worked with Peter Dawson in York to design this document. He gave permission for Angela Jensen in Swindon to amend and develop it. This amended version is the one that we now include. We would like to thank both Peter and Angela for their work and for permission to use the document in this book.

We have noted where we have omitted certain parts as they appear elsewhere in this book.

In addition, the LEA provided an Appendix comprising blank proforma.

How Can We Get Better?

School Improvement Planning for the 21st Century

Working together to make a difference

Acknowledgements

The guidance in this document is based on the model of school planning so well described by Brent Davies and Linda Ellison in *Strategic Direction and Development of the School* (1999). We would like to thank Brent, now Director of the International Leadership Centre at the University of Hull, for his support in the development of this guidance and his inspirational work with senior managers, governors and advisers in Swindon. Thanks also to colleagues in the City of York education department for permission to use their material as a basis for this document and the headteachers and governors who have worked on the various drafts of this guidance and provided invaluable feedback. We believe this document will be an effective tool for raising pupils' achievement and improving school effectiveness.

Contents

1. School Improvement Planning: Is it worth it?

It is important to distinguish between the plan itself and the process of planning. The challenge is to develop planning processes that get to grips with the real needs of the school and produce the goods.

The model of school improvement planning in this document combines the best of current practice with the facility to make preparations for the future.

The three strands of Futures Thinking, Strategy and Action Planning are all elements of current approaches to school improvement planning.

This model enables planning for aspects of school life that are stable and predictable.

This model enables a school to increase its capacity to respond to an uncertain future.

This model is not hierarchical or limited to a particular planning cycle.

The three strands of Futures Thinking, Strategy and Action Planning can occur at the same time. You can enter this planning framework at any point, depending on your school's need in the improvement planning process.

2. The Swindon Model for School Improvement Planning: Will it work better?

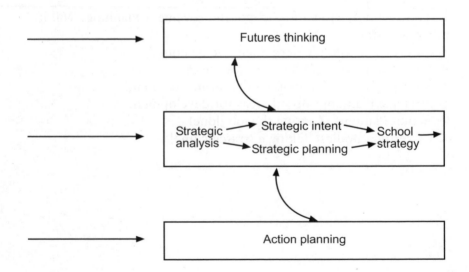

An alternative to the traditional, incremental planning model would be one which encourages schools to develop:

- a futures perspective – a means of expressing how they are going to tackle the major challenges of the next few years
- strategy formulation
- short-term planning, detailing how targets are to be met in the short term – action planning.

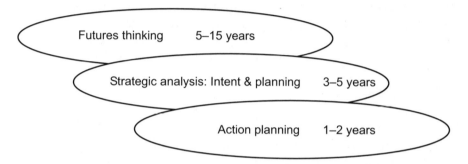

Futures thinking   5–15 years

Strategic analysis: Intent & planning   3–5 years

Action planning   1–2 years

Futures Thinking

Looking forward, outside the school, to develop perspectives of how the school may need to change to meet the challenges of the future.

This links with the school's vision and aims.

Strategic Analysis

Analysing information and building a strategic view.

Strategic Intent

Building capability and capacity to move the school forward. Planning more related to changing the culture of the school and its capacity to deal with issues where there may not be complete understanding or agreement.

Strategic Planning

Providing a medium-term overview of how definable and predictable issues are going to be tackled.

Action Planning

Short-term and usually detailed planning that needs to occur in order to make sure that the job gets done.

3. Futures Thinking: Where might we be going?

We need to redesign schools to prepare pupils for the challenges of the 21st century. We will not get there solely by teachers working longer hours, exhorting pupils to work harder, planning in more detail and doing more and more of the same! Schools will need to change significantly if they are to meet the challenges such as:

- Increased specialisation and differentiation between schools
- Radical changes in teaching and learning patterns
- Significant changes in staffing patterns and conditions
- Increased opportunities for flexible lifelong learning

Futures Thinking:

- involves the school community stepping back from traditional ways of thinking and working and analysing broad global and educational trends which are likely to impact on education over the next 10 to 15 years
- enables schools to think about how they might need to change in order to meet the challenges of the future
- discovers some of the questions to ask rather than trying to find the answers.

It is just possible that we might see:

- Schools as 'learning resource centres' functioning as co-ordinators of learning for the whole community and working with a wide range of 'learning providers'
- Learning days rather than teaching days where the 'taught timetable' fits into a range of learning experiences rather than the other way round
- Flexible staffing developments with teachers changing roles throughout their career, flexible contracting and the increase in availability of 'para-professionals'
- Information communication technology developments dominating change so that more learning can occur away from school
- An amalgamation of the role of 'commercial' and 'educational' training providers
- Restructuring of local education through the concept of a 'college

of schools', may see schools working together as learning providers

- Professional staff development using the concept of global staff tutors through Internet advances
- School leaders may need to look beyond their own stakeholders for challenge and inspiration.

Conventional development planning techniques are unable to capitalise on 'Futures Thinking' because of the lack of detail and certainty. Futures Thinking leads naturally to Strategic Intent in which the capacity of a school to exploit future opportunities is developed.

Futures Thinking is not the same as 'vision'. Futures Thinking is a process which enables us to start asking the questions which help to develop the 'vision'.

Futures Thinking does not allow detailed and precise planning. This is because there is uncertainty about the nature of the changes or because the need to change may not be fully understood. However it does allow schools to build up capability and a capacity to understand trends and the nature of the changes that must be made.

Example of a secondary/primary futures thinking perspective:

Future aspect identified	Potential impact on the school	School response
1. Technology	Resourcing issue Training staff Keeping up to date with inventions Home learning	
2. Organisation of the year	Different pattern of school year	
3. Staffing	Changing role of support assistants Developing teachers' skills & competencies Take away routine tasks from teachers	Training Identify & support development Performance management must be effective
4. Resourcing schools	A mixture of private and public funding	Investigate different forms of funding
5. The learning day	An extension of school activities Review of homework	

4. Strategic Analysis: Where are we now?

Strategic Analysis is about:

- Collecting information
- Interpreting information to arrive at issues and priorities.

For the information to be of any use it needs to be:

- Focused on what is learned and how it is learned
- Drawn from sources within and beyond the school
- From the stakeholders in the school, i.e. pupils, parents, teachers, governors, and the community.

Strategic analysis is a key leadership competence. Leaders need to be good at it!

- Analysis tools should make sense of the data. They help to focus attention on:

  ° The current position of key factors in the life of the school
  ° Understanding what needs to be done
  ° Communicating what needs to be done.

- A range of techniques can be used to support strategic analysis.

The following table summarises three key areas for analysis.

Area	Information needed	Sources/techniques
Beyond the school	Local and national trends International trends Work-place needs FE/HE needs	Networking Professional and subject organisations Social & economic reports from the LEA Employer surveys FE/HE surveys
Views of school 'stakeholders'	Perceptions of quality of learning and provision	Preference surveys Demography Interviews Questionnaires Attendance levels
Standards and Quality	Strengths and weaknesses	Inspections Reviews Monitoring and evaluation Data evaluation Benchmarking

- **Strategic Analysis** provides a better understanding of the needs of the school and the environment in which the school operates. It does not indicate priorities or which strategy should be used.
- **Strategic Analysis** will give rise to a number of areas that will need to be tackled in the medium term.
- The School Leadership and Management Team will need to decide:
  - Which areas to tackle
  - How to tackle them.

- In prioritising issues it is worth considering the following:
  - How much does it impinge on pupils' learning?
  - Does it fit with our 'strengths' and the 'opportunities' available?
  - Does it help us minimise our weaknesses?
  - Does it fit with our aims?
  - Is it currently acceptable?
  - Will it cause too much stress?
  - Is it what the stakeholders expect us to do?
  - Will it cost too much?
  - Is it likely to be successful?
  - Are resources available?

- Where projects are fairly clearly defined, adequately resourced, likely to succeed and reasonably well understood, then a **Strategic Plan** can be drawn up.
- Where there is a lack of definition, inadequate resources, success is unsure or there is insufficient understanding of the issue, which is nevertheless important, then it is necessary to develop capability through **Strategic Intent**.

... and finally!

Prioritisation should allow a school to identify the issues it can tackle by drawing up a **Strategic Plan**. Other important issues can become part of the school's **Strategic Intent**, allowing capability to be built up over time.

5. Strategic Intent: Developing the means to an end

Strategic intent states that you know where you want to go but accepts that you don't know how to get there yet. What is needed is a process of building capability and capacity in the school to understand the dimensions of what needs to be done and how that can be achieved. (This contrasts with strategic planning where you know what you want to do and how to do it.)

A school, after a period of reflection and discussion, decided that it was necessary to build capability through the following Strategic Intents:

1. Develop a 'best is normal' culture for all staff and pupils
2. Establish independent learning strategies for staff and pupils
3. Extend and develop ICT capability for all staff and pupils
4. Improve the health of all staff and pupils
5. Improve communication
6. Reduce bureaucracy and paperwork.

When these strategic intents were set, few in the school knew how they were to be achieved! However, everyone agreed that they were important, that they needed to understand more about them and that they could shape the school for the future. Underpinning each of these strategic intents were capability-building measures designed to develop an understanding of the issues. When the school decided that sufficient understanding existed and/or the time was right, then it was possible to plan in these areas in sufficient detail that expectations of success could be high.

... and finally!

Whilst detailed planning may not always be possible, strategic intent may provide a 'steer' to day-to-day activities and a direction to how longer-term issues may need to develop. However, all schools will need to plan for immediate and medium-term issues.

(The document then presents the 'building capability' chart which forms part of Chapter Three on page 43.)

6. Strategic Planning: Broad areas for development

Strategic Planning is about:

- Focusing on what needs to be done to improve *outcomes for pupils*
- Addressing priorities where there is certainty and understanding
- Planning for the medium term, that is, up to 5 years
- Providing an overview of strategy rather than details of activities
- Identifying the timescale, leader and estimated costs
- Communicating to teachers, governors, parents and the LEA key medium-term developments and their expected effect on learning
- Directing the school improvement planning activities of departments within the school
- Providing a framework within which progress towards strategic targets can be monitored and evaluated, especially by school leaders and the Governing Body.

The Strategic Plan:

- Links, for each priority, targets for three important aspects of any issue:
  1. **What pupils achieve** – educational standards
  2. **How the school supports learning** – quality of education
  3. **How resources are made available to support learning** – management and efficiency.

Strategic Planning focuses on broad areas of development. It should not be cluttered with detail. Importantly it should describe and provide the basis for monitoring the strategic direction of the school by school leaders and governors. Detailed planning, often describing how a particular department or teacher intends to interpret whole-school targets, is the concern of **Action Planning.**

The choice of priorities for the strategic plan will evolve from ongoing school self-evaluation. The **Swindon LEA guidelines on School Self Evaluation** provide a framework with features of effective schools organised under the headings of :

- Professional leadership and management
- The learning environment
- Purposeful teaching and learning and effective relationships
- High expectations
- Monitoring progress
- Pupils' rights and responsibilities

- Home–school partnership
- The learning organisation.

The guidance document then shows examples of strategic plans for a primary and a secondary school, similar to the ones which we show in Chapter Three on pages 46 and 47. In the LEA guidance, one strand of each plan is highlighted (literacy in the primary school plan and numeracy in the secondary plan) so that this strand can be traced through action plans, subject plans and individual staff and pupil action plans.

7. Action Planning: Getting the job done!

Action Planning:

- Is about achieving targets and meeting expectations and
- Is largely led by the whole-school Strategic Plan.

A number of action plans will be drawn up to address:

- Whole-school targets
- Departmental or area targets
- Class targets or expectations
- Teacher targets or expectations
- Pupil targets or expectations.

Key priorities, for example, raising standards in literacy, will involve setting targets for the whole school, separate key stages, year groups, classes and individual pupils. The resulting action plans will illustrate how departments or subject leaders are planning to address the whole-school target in their area.

The choice of activities may be influenced by the school's Strategic Intent.

Action planning:

- Is focused on raising pupil achievement
- May require departments, areas or individual teachers to reinterpret whole-school targets to take account of their own particular context
- Is short term (1 to 2 years)
- Describes key tasks to get the job done
- Is developmental; the planning is never finished until the job is finished!
- Should include the following steps:
  - Making general targets more specific. The focus of action planning is increasing pupil achievement
  - Involving stakeholders – everyone at all levels!
  - Identifying and prioritising tasks
  - Allocating resources
  - Communicating
  - Monitoring progress
  - Evaluation.

Action Plans come in different shapes and sizes. However they should record the above processes.

... and finally!

Action Planning is not intended to be bureaucratic or time consuming. If it becomes so, stop it! Its job is to ensure that important jobs get done.

The LEA guidance document then shows secondary and primary action plans as follows:

- *School action plans to meet whole-school targets*
- *Science action plan to meet whole-school targets*
- *Science action plan to develop science as a subject area*
- *Individual staff action plans*
- *Pupil action plans*

We have omitted these for reasons of space. They are very similar to the ones which we show on pages 95–103 of Chapter Five and in our previous book (Davies and Ellison 1999).

8. Governing Bodies: Taking a strategic line!

The Governing Body should play a largely strategic role in overseeing the work of the school. This includes:

- Setting up a strategic planning framework to enable the school to move forward
- Developing and reviewing its aims and objectives
- Setting policies and targets for achieving the objectives
- Reviewing progress and the strategic direction of the school in the light of advice
- Acting as a 'critical friend' to the headteacher by providing support and advice and asking questions.

Effective school improvement planning is concerned with identifying:

- Which aspects of pupil achievement need to improve ... and by how much
- What the school intends to do to achieve the improvement ... and by when
- Who will lead the improvement
- How much it will cost
- How the plan is monitored and evaluated
- Which priorities should be given priority!

Through discussion and debate with the School Leadership and Management Team, the Governing Body should:

- Identify and agree priorities and choose options to inform action plans
- Understand the context in which the pupils and teachers operate
- Agree a strategic plan addressing broad areas for development
- Agree a budget to meet the needs of the strategic plan and the action plan
- Monitor and evaluate progress towards targets from a range of evidence including:
  - ° feedback from the headteacher and staff to governors linked to particular priorities or subjects, governor committees and the whole governing body
  - ° national, local and school data on pupil standards and progress
  - ° reports from advisers, consultants and inspectors.

A well-crafted School Improvement Plan makes this manageable.

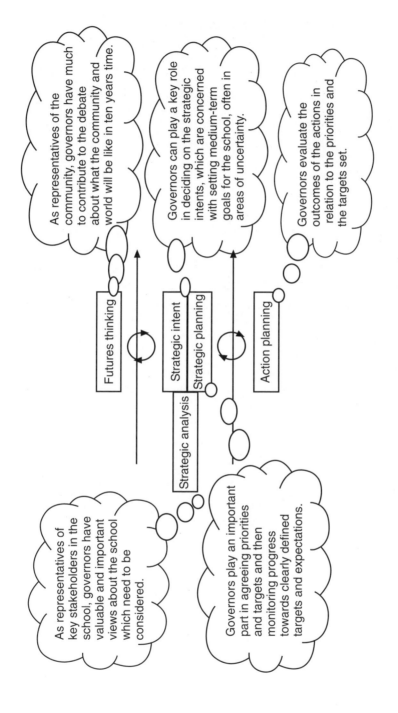

As representatives of the community, governors have much to contribute to the debate about what the community and world will be like in ten years time.

Governors can play a key role in deciding on the strategic intents, which are concerned with setting medium-term goals for the school, often in areas of uncertainty.

Governors evaluate the outcomes of the actions in relation to the priorities and the targets set.

Futures thinking

Strategic intent

Strategic planning

Strategic analysis

Action planning

As representatives of key stakeholders in the school, governors have valuable and important views about the school which need to be considered.

Governors play an important part in agreeing priorities and targets and then monitoring progress towards clearly defined targets and expectations.

The Governors' Role in School Improvement Planning

Appendix – Proforma

Here, we set out the proforma for the different strands of the plan. We have worked with a great many schools, LEAs and senior staff and we are very conscious of the fact that one size does not fit all. We therefore present these proforma as a stimulus to thinking in schools. We would expect that some schools would adapt these, others would combine some of them with their existing proforma and so on. In Chapters Six, Seven and Eight we showed case examples of the ways in which our ideas have been developed by particular schools and LEAs to illustrate this.

A school improvement plan should have four components as follows:

1. Introduction or context statement — the nature and dimensions of the school – age range of pupils, location etc.

2. Futures perspective — report of futures dialogue and perspectives developed in the school

3. Strategic dimension — i) strategic intent statement
   ii) strategic plan

4. Operational dimension — short-term action plans at a number of levels

Introduction or context statement

(This would be one page explaining about the type of school, its physical and social location and any major issues and relationships.)

Futures Perspective

	Area chosen	Potential impact on the school	School response
1.			
2.			
3.			
4.			
5.			

Strategic Dimension

Strategic intent

Strategic intents for the school

Intent	Capability-building measures	Outcomes

Strategic plan

Strategic planning area	Strategic planning activities	Time frame 3–5 years	Costs	Responsibility	Monitoring	Evaluation
Learning outcomes: pupil progress & achievement						
Support for the quality of learning & teaching processes						
Leadership & management arrangements						
Physical & financial resources, school structure & organisation						

Operational Dimension

Whole-school action plan for (year)

Target	Responsibility	Cost	Desired Outcome	Completed by	Reviewed by
1.					
2.					
3.					
4.					
5.					

Area plans to meet whole-school action plan (*year*)

Whole-school target	Actions/Tasks/ Strategies	Responsibility	Who involved?	Cost	Inset	Desired outcome (how know achieved?)	Completed by	Monitored by

Area-specific action plans (year)

Area target	Actions/Tasks/Strategies	Responsibility	Who involved?	Cost	Inset	Desired outcome (how know achieved?)	Completed by	Monitored by
1.								
2.								
3.								
4.								
5.								
6.								
7.								

Individual staff plans

<table>
<tr><td colspan="4">

PERFORMANCE REVIEW / INDIVIDUAL STAFF TARGETS

</td></tr>
<tr><td colspan="2">

NAME:

Subject/Year/KS Group:

</td><td colspan="2">

PERIOD:

Reporting to:

</td></tr>
<tr><td>**Overview/Context Questions**</td><td>**Individual Specific Targets**</td><td>**By when**</td><td>**Rev by**</td></tr>
<tr><td>

Phase One:

1. What contribution did you make to whole-school plans last year?

2. What contribution did you make to your area of responsibility (subject, year group, Key Stage etc.)?

Phase Two:

1. What contribution will you make to whole-school plans next year?

2. What contribution will you make to your area of responsibility (subject, year group, Key Stage etc.)?

Phase Three

What support do you need to achieve your targets for next year?

</td><td>

1.

2.

3.

4.

5.

6.

</td><td></td><td></td></tr>
</table>

Targets should relate to: whole school
area
pupil
own CPD

Pupil action plans – Primary

PUPIL PERSONAL ACTION PLAN	
NAME	**ACTION PLAN FOR PERIOD**
CLASS	....

What I would like to become better at	How do you think you could do this?	Who needs to help you?	What do you need to help you to do this?	When will you do it by?	Teacher comment
In school					
Out of school					

Targets could relate to: achievement in learning
extra-curricular activity
behaviour

PUPIL PERSONAL ACTION PLAN

NAME	ACTION PLAN FOR PERIOD
CLASS	CLASS TEACHER/PERSONAL TUTOR

Target	Action planned	By when?	Comment
Achievement in learning			
Extra-curricular activity			
Community contribution			
Behaviour			

Targets should relate to: achievement in learning
extra-curricular activity
community contribution
behaviour

References

Adey, P. and Shayer, M. (1994) *Raising Standards: Cognitive Intervention and Academic Achievement*, London: Routledge.

Barber, M. (1996) *The Learning Game*, London: Golancz.

Barker, G. (2003) 'Reengineering teaching and learning in the primary school', in B. Davies and J. West-Burnham *Handbook of Educational Leadership and Management*, London: Pearson.

Boisot, M. (1995) 'Preparing for turbulence', in *Developing Strategic Thought*, B. Garratt (ed.), London: McGraw-Hill.

Bowman, C. and Asch, D. (1987) *Strategic Management*, Basingstoke: Macmillan.

Caldwell, B.J. (1997b) 'A gestalt for the new millennium' in B. Davies and L. Ellison *School Leadership for the 21st Century,* London: Routledge.

Caldwell, B.J. and Spinks, J.M. (1988) *The Self-Managing School*, London: Falmer Press.

Caldwell, B.J. and Spinks, J.M. (1992) *Leading the Self-Managing School*, London: Falmer Press.

Caldwell, B.J. and Spinks, J.M. (1998) *Beyond the Self-Managing School*, London: Falmer Press.

Davies, B. (2002a) 'Rethinking strategy and strategic leadership in schools', paper given at The National College for School Leadership, 1st Invitational International Conference: An International Future: Learning from Best Practice Worldwide, Nottingham, October.

Davies, B. (2002b) 'Rethinking schools and school leadership for the twenty-first century: changes and challenges', *International Journal of Education Management*, 16 (4), pp. 196–206.

Davies, B. and Davies, B.J. (2003) 'Strategy and planning in schools', in B. Davies and J. West-Burnham (eds) *Handbook of Educational Leadership and Management*, London: Pearson.

Davies, B. and Ellison, L. (1997a) *School Leadership for the 21st Century*, London: Routledge.

Davies, B. and Ellison, L. (1997b) *Strategic Marketing for Schools*, London: Pitman.

Davies, B. and Ellison, L. (1999) *Strategic Direction and Development of the School*, London: Routledge.

Davies, B. and Hentschke, G. (2002) 'Changing resource and organisational patterns – the challenge of resourcing education in the 21st century', *Journal of Educational Change*, 3 (2), pp. 135–59.

Davies, B.J. (2003) Washingborough School Planning document.

Dent, H.S. (1995) *Jobshock,* New York: St Martin's Press.

DES (1988) *The Education Reform Act*, London: HMSO.

DfEE (1996) *Setting Targets to Raise Standards: A Survey of Good Practice*, London: DfEE.

DfEE (1997) *From Targets to Action*, London: DfEE.

DfEE (2001) NPQH Unit 'Strategic Direction and Development of the School', Unit 1.3 'School Development Planning' Section 7 ~ Strategic Management, pp. 43–5.

Drucker, P. (1993) *Post-capitalist Society*, New York: Harper Business.

Drucker P. (1995) *Managing in a Time of Great Change*, Oxford: Butterworth Heinemann.

Ellison, L. (2002) 'Strategic leadership', paper given at The National College for School Leadership, 1st Invitational International Conference: An International Future: Learning from Best Practice Worldwide, Nottingham, October.

Fidler, B. (2002) *Strategic Management for School Development*, London: Paul Chapman Publishing.

Fullan, M. (1993) *Change Forces – Probing the Depths of Educational Reform*, London: Falmer Press.

Gardner, H. (1999) *Intelligence Reframed – Multiple Intelligences for the 21st Century*, New York: Basic Books.

Gates, B. (1995) *The Road Ahead*, London: Viking.

Glatter, R., Woods, P. and Bagley, C. (1995) *Diversity, Differentiation and Hierarchy: School Choice and Parental Preferences*, ESRC/CEPAM Invitation Seminar, Milton Keynes, 7–8 June.

Gorard, S. (1999) '"Well. That about wraps it up for school choice research": a state of the art review', *School Leadership and Management,* 19 (1), pp 25–47.

Hamel, G. and Prahalad, C.K. (1989) 'Strategic intent', *Harvard Business Review*, May/June.

Hamel, G. and Prahalad, C.K. (1994) *Competing for the Future*. Boston: Harvard Business School Press.

Hammer, M. and Champy, J. (1993) *Reengineering the Corporation*, New York: HarperCollins.

Hammer, M. and Stanton, S.A. (1995) *The Reengineering Revolution – A Handbook,* New York: Harper Business.

Handy, C. (1990) *The Age of Unreason*, London: Arrow Books.

Handy, C. (1994) *The Empty Raincoat: Making Sense of the Future*, London: Hutchinson.

Hargreaves, A. (2000) 'The three dimensions of educational reform', paper presented at the Launch Conference of the Global Alliance for School Leadership, Nottingham, May.

Hargreaves, D. (1997) 'A road to the learning society', *School Leadership & Management*, 17 (1), pp. 9–21.

Husbands, C. (2001) 'Labour must learn to let go', *Times Educational Supplement,* 13 April, p. 15.

Johnson, G. and Scholes, K. (1993) *Exploring Corporate Strategy*, 3rd edn, London: Prentice Hall.

Leadbeater, C. (1999) *Living on Thin Air – the New Economy,* London: Viking.

Leat, D. (1999) 'Rolling the stone uphill: teachers' development and the implementation of thinking skills programmes', *Oxford Review of Education*, 25 (3), pp. 387–403.

Lewis, J. (1997) 'From a blank sheet of paper', in B. Davies and J. West-Burnham (eds) *Reengineering and Total Quality in Schools*, London: Pitman.

Local Government Association (2000) *The Rhythms of Schooling*, London: Local Government Association.

Moe, M.T., Bailey, K. and Lau, R. (1999) *The Book of Knowledge: Investing in the Growing Education and Training Industry*, New York: Merrill Lynch.

OFSTED (2001) Action Planning for School Improvement; www.ofsted.gov.uk accessed 21 July 2002.

Perkins, D. (1992) *Smart Schools*, New York: The Free Press.

Porter, M. (1980) *Competitive Strategy*, New York: The Free Press.

Reich, R. (1992) *The Work of Nations*, New York: Vintage Books.

Smith, A. (1996) *Accelerated Learning in Classrooms*, Stafford: Network Press.

Taberrer, R. (1997) Lecture given to the Yorkshire and Humberside Region of BEMAS, Sheffield, 25 June.

Thrupp, M. (2002) 'The school leadership literature in managerialist times: exploring the problem of textual apologism', paper presented at ESRC Seminar Series – Challenging the orthodoxy of school leadership: towards new theoretical Perspectives, University of Warwick, 28 November 2002.

Tsaikkiros, A. and Pashiardis, P. (2002) 'Strategic planning and education: the case of Cyprus', *International Journal of Education Management*, 16 (1), pp. 6–17.

Williamson, O.E. (1987) *The Economic Institutions of Capitalism*, New York: The Free Press.

Williamson, O.E. and Masten, S.E. (eds) (1999) *The Economics of Transactions Costs*, London: Edward Elgar Publishers.

Wise, D. (2003) 'Reengineering in the secondary school', in B. Davies and J. West-Burnham (eds) *Handbook of Educational Leadership and Management*, London: Pearson.

Index